ON BECOMING
nuyoricans

Studies in the
Postmodern Theory of Education

Joe L. Kincheloe and Shirley R. Steinberg
General Editors

Vol. 194

PETER LANG
New York • Washington, D.C./Baltimore • Bern
Frankfurt am Main • Berlin • Brussels • Vienna • Oxford

Angela Anselmo
& Alma Rubal-Lopez

ON BECOMING
Nuyoricans

PETER LANG
New York • Washington, D.C./Baltimore • Bern
Frankfurt am Main • Berlin • Brussels • Vienna • Oxford

Library of Congress Cataloging-in-Publication Data

Anselmo, Angela.
On becoming Nuyoricans / Angela Anselmo, Alma Rubal-Lopez.
p. cm. — (Counterpoints; vol. 194)
Includes bibliographical references.
1. Puerto Ricans—Education—New York (State)—New York—Case studies.
2. Puerto Ricans—Cultural assimilation—New York (State)—New York—
Case studies. 3. Multicultural education—New York (State)—
New York—Case studies. 4. Rubal-Lopez, Alma.
5. Anselmo, Angela. I. Anselmo, Angela. II. Title.
III. Counterpoints (New York, N.Y.); v. 194.
LC2698.N48R83   371.82968'7295—dc21   2003008142
ISBN 0-8204-5520-2
ISSN 1058-1634

Bibliographic information published by **Die Deutsche Bibliothek**.
Die Deutsche Bibliothek lists this publication in the "Deutsche
Nationalbibliografie"; detailed bibliographic data is available
on the Internet at http://dnb.ddb.de/.

Cover design by Lisa Barfield

The paper in this book meets the guidelines for permanence and durability
of the Committee on Production Guidelines for Book Longevity
of the Council of Library Resources.

© 2005 Peter Lang Publishing, Inc., New York
275 Seventh Avenue, 28th Floor, New York, NY 10001
www.peterlangusa.com

Printed in the United States of America

For our parents
who did the best they could

Contents

Introduction

This book takes a very personal look at two sisters' views of their experiences growing up in the South Bronx and how they negotiated an often hostile, racist, and confusing environment. Both sisters are currently faculty members of the City University of New York and both have attained doctorates in bilingual developmental psychology. The unlikelihood that two Puerto Rican females, from the same family from Patterson Projects in the South Bronx during the 1950s, would have taken such paths has led to a lifetime of people posing questions about issues regarding their reasons for pursuing their education. At times they have found themselves pondering the same issues and trying to shed light on the forces in their lives that have led them to make such choices. The result has been the creation of this book. Not surprisingly, education and their experiences in school become focal points in this inquiry.

Today, there are more positive media images of Puerto Ricans than ever before. Jennifer Lopez, Jimmy Smits, Ricky Martin, and Marc Anthony have become part of the American entertainment scene. Names like Trinidad Lopez, Juan Gonzalez, Bernie Williams, and Roberto and Sandy Lomar are familiar to sports fans. While they do help to bring attention to the fact that Puerto Ricans are a formidable group in American society, such representations do little to inform America about Puerto Rico's culture and people. What does the average American know about Puerto Ricans? Puerto Ricans come from a relatively small island in the Caribbean Sea—only 100 miles long and approximately 30 miles wide. Yet Puerto Ricans, after Mexican Americans, represent the largest Latino group in the United States. Their greatest concentration is found along the East Coast, with New York leading as the city with the largest number.

The migration of Puerto Ricans to the United States is the by-product of the island's colonial relationship with this nation. In 1898 the Treaty of Paris that ended the Spanish-American War granted the Island of Puerto Rico to the United States from Spain. While the legality of this appropriation is questionable, it nonetheless paved the way for a relationship between the two nations of unequal economic, military, and political power. Within a few decades following the American invasion, Puerto Rico was transformed from a nation with a diversified subsistence economy that produced tobacco, coffee, cattle, and sugar to a single-crop sugar economy. This propelled the first wave of Puerto Rican migrants to the United States during the 1920s and 1930s. Subsequent political and economic policies of the United States on the island propelled the next and largest phase of migration to the United States from 1946 to 1964. It is that period of the Puerto Rican migration that this book focuses on. This era is known as "the great migration" and also refers to the Puerto Rican diaspora because of the great numbers of persons who left the island and settled in various parts of this country. The bulk of the population, however, settled in New York in parts of East Harlem, the South Bronx, and the Lower East Side.

Unlike the migration of other populations who came from other hemispheres and arrived at our shores on ships, Puerto Ricans originated from the same hemisphere, arrived by plane, and left their homeland because of an economic situation that was directly due to American economic policy on the island. Furthermore, unlike other immigrants who came in search of becoming Americans, Puerto Ricans were already American citizens. Puerto Rican differed from other immigrants and their fellow citizens in other ways. Racially, the Puerto Rican is a mixture of Taino Indian, Spanish, and African. Linguistically, Spanish is the mother tongue and Catholicism is the principal religion. Hence, the migration and the process of "Americanization" for Puerto Ricans, who also have strong allegiance to their island, have not been easy or painless.

Both sisters were part of the first generation of Puerto Ricans born and raised in New York during the 1950s and 1960s. Their generation paved the way for subsequent immigrant populations from the Caribbean, Latin America, and other non-European countries that settled in New York City. This generation of Puerto Ricans born in New York, also referred to as "Nuyoricans," was undoubtedly critical in helping to define issues of race, assimilation, and equity never before confronted by immigrants (African Americans notwithstanding) who were not white Europeans in a society that defined itself as a "melting pot."

Their personal perspectives on race, religion, education, images in the media, return migration to Puerto Rico, language, and their parents will be explored. This study should help readers to better understand that generation, living at a time in American society that lacked a precedent for handling such issues, and its impact on subsequent populations of non-European white immigrants.

Part I of the book consists of a series of childhood experiences told from each sister's own perspective. Thus, what emerges is a recollection of how each sibling saw that particular segment of her life. The second half of the book examines critical issues related to community, home, class, values, motivation, and identity that have played a role in molding who these two women are today.

In essence, this book provides an important look at a pivotal period in American society as depicted in their narratives and an analysis of their recollections.

Introduction of Alma by Angie

In gathering my thoughts for my introduction of my younger sister, Alma, many things have come to mind.

First is the obvious: Alma is not only my sister but also my friend. This is not always the case with siblings. She is a loving wife and mother, a loyal friend, a creative and inspiring educator, an effective and responsible administrator, a caring counselor, and an insightful scholar. Alma is a problem solver, a great cook, and has been known to be an enthusiastic party animal. She can tell a great story and loves to make others laugh. But do not mess with her or her loved ones. She has a sharp tongue and can be a daunting and unforgiving enemy. She has the uncanny ability to strike at the most vulnerable spots.

On the other hand, Alma is very fair, intelligent, and rational. She readily sees both sides of an argument and can be won over with logic and clarity. She is a highly principled person of great integrity and honesty who can be a bit of an idealist.

Also obvious is the fact that excluding my father, I have known Alma longer than any other living human being. This does not mean that I know her better than anyone else, but the length of our connection as sisters spans five decades and has been a constant since she was born. The reverse is also true. She has known me longer than anyone else, at least in this lifetime. We have witnessed and participated in many events and milestones in each other's lives.

We shared the same home, parents, culture, era, relatives, and even education. We were not as close as children as we are now as adults. We were enrolled in the same graduate programs for our first and second master's degrees as well as our doctorates in bilingual developmental psychology. We took the exact same courses, had the same instructors, usually sat next to each other, and studied for and took the same exams together; we even defended our doctoral dissertations within one week of each other. Currently, we both have the same employer: The City University of New York. Alma is a professor at Brooklyn College and I am an administrator at Baruch College.

We became mothers within one year of each other, delivered by the same obstetrician. Our children have also shared many times together. Thus, we have a lot in common.

Despite this, I feel that Alma and I are different in what developmental psychologists call temperament. I once heard it said that when breeding bulls that will later be utilized in the bullring, only those who fight back when prodded are selected. The bull that pulls back or retreats is eliminated. I think Alma is a fighter and I am more of a retreater. She has taken on many tough battles in her life in the name of justice and for what she believes is the right thing. In the process, she has ruffled many feathers. Examples include her work in Attica (the maximum security state prison in upstate New York), where she served as the first female educational counselor and was instrumental in effecting changes in a very dense bureaucratic culture, and her work in community organizations and even corporate America, where she has always left her mark. Alma is the fighter of the two.

Alma is more grounded and in touch with the real world. I am more gullible. Alma needs more time and evidence before trusting in people. I tend to fall in love with people and get disappointed at a later time. As a child I was either in awe of the nuns or terrified of them. Alma never took them very seriously. Part of her skepticism of religion, heaven, and hell was her need to have tangible evidence of an afterlife or the infallibility of the pope. Believing everything that the nuns told us was not her idea of faith.

Even though she is two years younger, she was the source of much of the vital information that shook up my childhood, such as the "facts of life" and that there was no Santa Claus.

Alma was more normal in the sense that she did things that were typical for our age group. She was much more a product of the '60s and '70s than I was. She did the conventional things that young people of our generation did. She dated in high school while I did research with a spectrophotometer. She worked part-time and went to rock concerts and parties and "sets," as they were called in those days, while I was busy studying, praying, and doing volunteer work. She dreamed of having her own home; I aspired to go to heaven. She wanted to be a lawyer; I wanted to be a saint. In retrospect I was always out of sync with my peers. I was married while I went to college and started dating after I got divorced and out of graduate school. It seemed to me that I was always playing catch-up with my generation. Alma was more on track.

I was as skinny as a beanpole without much of a female shape until my twenties. Alma was a knockout as teenager. She had what was referred to as a killer body. I was *la flaca* (the skinny one) and she was known as *la que esta buena* (the hot or attractive one). Because Alma developed physically into a woman at an early age, she often used my I.D. So I even looked younger than she did.

Alma has often expressed to me the difficulty of having had me as a sister while growing up because of the many expectations placed on her by my parents and teachers. She has shared with me that she thought I was more intelligent than she was. I did get better grades, but I have never felt more intelligent than Alma. I am in awe of how she thinks. She has a sense of the big picture. She has a "macro" perspective. She looks at things from a more historical, political, sociological, and cross-cultural standpoint. I am more "micro." I am concerned with the personal, psychological, and spiritual dimensions. Nevertheless, this feeling of somehow being less intelligent did not stop her from attempting graduate work. She forged ahead despite her insecurities.

On the other hand, many of my childhood experiences such as the ethnic wounding or sexual violations I underwent haunted me into my adult years. Somehow, I tend to internalize and bury my fear and pain and it often paralyzes me. I think Alma is more likely to externalize, to act it out or confront it.

Alma has fewer problems expressing emotions such as anger and fewer problems with creating boundaries with people. Thus, she also takes more risks in her relationships by being real and telling people things that they do not want to hear. Sometimes this has backfired in her life. I am very afraid of hurting people and of being an object of their anger, so I am less authentic in many instances and perceived as more diplomatic.

Alma is a doer and thinker. When she isn't parenting, teaching, administering, or counseling, she is writing articles, grants, and proposals. When she isn't doing, she is thinking about what she will be doing next or what others should be doing. She forever has a possible conference to which she thinks I should submit a proposal. I would never have attempted a doctorate if Alma had not talked me into it. I had the stronger academic record, but getting a doctorate was a dream I had given up on. Even the writing of this book was an idea she had had for quite some time. I, on the other hand, never imagined that such a thing was possible. Alma has endless ideas for possible other projects as well. Her future seems full of work. These days I am more of a person who wants to *be* rather than *do*.

We both love to learn, but my learning is not very organized or goal oriented. It seems to center around inner growth and spirituality. Not all but much of Alma's continual learning is connected to her professional development and career. She is a professor and she keeps up-to-date in her profession. I do not feel that I even have a career. I have ended up being an administrator almost by accident. It was not a conscious decision and certainly not motivated by a burning desire to be a boss. Alma is more conscious of her strengths and weaknesses and has made more conscious choices in her life concerning her vocation.

Writing this book with her has given me the opportunity to get to know her better. I was unaware of how very sensitive Alma is and how much she suffered with the divorce of our parents. I was so wrapped up in my own problems as a youngster that I was oblivious to her pain. The experience has made us closer and I appreciate her more as the great being that she is. For this I will always be grateful.

Introduction of Angie by Alma

Angie is my only sibling. She is two years older than I am, although I have always felt that I am the older of the two of us. It is very difficult to write about Angie without seeming to be extremely biased or untruthful or to have a distorted view because she is an exceptional person who at times has made my life very difficult because of her exceptional qualities. As I tell my students when speaking of my childhood experiences, for the first sixteen years of my life I shared my bedroom with a sister who is a combination of Mother Teresa and Albert Einstein. What can you say of a sibling who spent her childhood preparing for entrance into heaven and achieving academically? In both domains Angie has succeeded. She is not only one of the smartest persons I know but is also one of the nicest. She is unusual. Luckily for me, her perfection came to an end when she eloped with a man eighteen years her senior and dropped out of Barnard College in her freshman year. Nonetheless, my parents soon got over this and in their eyes, and rightfully so, she is still the better of both of us.

For those who are shocked and feel sorry for me, I plead to spare your feelings. I am very comfortable being the one with all the flaws. Mediocrity can be quite commodious. It has its advantages. Nothing is expected of me, and my small successes are celebrated. My parents are in awe of the fact that I have attained what I have and shocked at the fact that Angie did not graduate from an Ivy League college despite offers and acceptance into several such colleges.

True, I have had to deal with self-esteem issues, but they have not stood in the way of my doing what I wish to do. Any self-esteem issues have been due to the very high bar because I was being compared to Angie, and a feeling that I was never doing enough, rather than because I was incapable of succeeding. Acceptance of my secondary status has provided me with many benefits, including having the freedom to argue with my father, not having to cater to his every wish, and not feeling compelled to clean his apartment when I visit him. Angie, on the other hand, has had a standard that she has set and that has been set for her which is higher and more difficult to reach. She is like the Martha Stewart of the Puerto Ricans. Not because of her cooking and crafts, but because of the absence of any great detectable blemish. More recently, Martha has come under fire as the media has unraveled her personal self, and Angie will in turn be unraveled as I introduce her.

While Angie is as perfect as one can be, she does have her flaws. We are not what we appear. As a child, she had the ability to get me so angry that we would get into physical fights. These were not small hitting or shoving incidents, but actual fistfights in which we would really hurt one another. During these fights, she would transform herself into a demon. I never understood how a skinny kid who looked malnourished could have the strength that she had or the anger that would cause her to inflict such pain. When she was not in her demon mode, Angie was as saintly as one can be. Even in pictures of her first communion, Angie's face radiates saintliness—unlike my picture, in which I appear with a smile that borders on laughing.

The greatest difference between both of us lies in our reactions to religion and spirituality. These two are of most importance in Angie's life, while in mine they are present but not to the degree that Angie has incorporated them into hers. While this seems to be a rather reasonable difference between sisters, it has affected both of us in unexpected ways. As a child Angie was ridden with guilt and fear of hell and mortal sin, which was in turn witnessed and internalized by me. I remember her dragging me to Sunday mass in the midst of a snowstorm because not attending would place us in a state of mortal sin. However, I also remember her deciding not to continue to go to mass, and my following her lead in this matter. In many ways she has influenced my spiritual path.

Luckily, I reached Piaget's stage of formal operations, in which logical thought emerges, and my illogical guilt ceased. For Angie, guilt continued despite her age and has plagued her ever since. This has resulted in her being someone who cannot say no to people, someone who is forever trying to please, and a person who blames herself for everything, resulting in Angie being taken advantage of by many. My reaction to this has evolved from coming to her defense and fighting for her as I have done in the past, to witnessing her allowance of such treatment and separating myself from the situation. At times while Angie has turned the other cheek, I have been in the background encouraging her to throw a punch. At times I have even found myself throwing that punch. Not surprisingly, Angie is the sweet one while I am her bitchy sister. Angie's qualities make her a very good friend. Nonetheless, her inability to say no places demands on her that are often unreasonable by persons who are supposed to be friends. There are many times that I have chosen to distance myself because she does not have the room for one more demand. Nonetheless, we both know that whatever happens we are here for one another.

We have led each other through many journeys. Angie's have been numerous. While some include her period as a young woman married to a professor of English as well as her time spent as a disco queen, those journeys that are most representative of who she is are those having to do with spirituality or self-improvement. These include her wanting to be a nun, going through est training, biofeedback, visualization, vegetarianism, taking part in "A Course in Miracles," attending Unity services, dragging me to religious services in a small congregation in the West Village, reading practically every self-help book, being ordained as an interfaith minister, and, lastly, being involved in Essence Training. While I have at her encouragement also taken part in many of these adventures, I can honestly say that the passion, intensity, and commitment with which she has approached each one is daunting to me. None of these activities, which include such things as a three-day process that required little sleep and few bathroom breaks in order to "get it" (as in the case of the est training), altering my diet, meditation, or opening my chakras, have been life-altering for me. In contrast, after undergoing each process, Angie has emerged a transformed person and a believer, at least until her next adventure.

Angie has been a true spiritual adventurer. She has pushed the line farther and farther. Her many adventures have allowed me to witness things that I would never have witnessed. More importantly, what has emerged is a sister, daughter, friend, mother, and professional who sets a standard that few can reach but that many recognize and aspire to emulate.

Part I

The Story

Chapter One

Beginnings
Children of the Projects

Angie

The memories of my childhood center on feelings and images involving love and fear, the roles of men and women, and issues of safety and violence. Although the projects in the South Bronx where Alma and I spent our early childhood provided a sense of community because it was a place where we were accepted and, on many occasions, that offered a great deal of fun for two curious little girls seeking adventure, my most vivid recollections of that time are of moments of tremendous vulnerability.

Illness was the central theme in our household: my asthma and my mother's arthritis. Just beneath the very comforting smells of ethnic foods that filled our apartment on any given afternoon was the unsettling scent of the Ben Gay that I used to rub into my mother's knees and shoulders. This situation, coupled with the overwhelming odor of Vicks VapoRub, which was used on me for everything from a congested chest and blocked nasal passages to minor cuts and bruises, was a reminder to us all that for each moment of joy there was pain and uncertainty waiting in the wings to abruptly snatch away the happiness.

There is the memory of *Agua Florida*, an aromatic astringent that was mixed with herbs and used to bring down fevers and alleviate headaches and sore muscles. It was a home remedy created by *Abuelita* (grandmother) Panchita, my father's mother, who was an expert in herbology. Panchita was the first registered nurse trained in Puerto Rico, and she is someone whom I am convinced had healing hands—strong, smooth, and medicinal. Her *sobos*, or rubdowns, were magical.

At an early age I became aware of the fragility, betrayal, and wonder of the human body. When I was seven years of age, I had an emergency appendectomy at one of the worst hospitals in the Bronx, St. Francis. I still have a hideous scar that transports me back to the day that I was held down by four nurses while the doctor removed my stitches. An infection had set in. I was absolutely terrified of being wheeled into the operating room and having my mouth and nose covered by that mask. The recovery was a lonely one. I spent over a month in that wretched hospital, alone and without family and friends, crying myself to sleep every night while a tube drained the pus from my wound.

Then there was my mother. As a child, I would go through her photo albums and see shots of her, a young Carmen Bryan, dressed in a ball gown, sitting in a cockpit, posing "à la Betty Gable" on a beach. Her smile in those photos was luminous and warm and absorbing. There were society clippings from a Georgia newspaper, recounting parties with a mention of the lovely Miss Bryan. Along with her photo albums were mementos of a trip to the 1939 New York World's Fair and leftovers of her wardrobe in the closet. The embroidered silk jackets, beaded evening dresses, velvet wraps, sequined bags, satin gloves, and hats with veils and ostrich feathers provided hard evidence of how magnificent she must have been. Then her world imploded and there were no more balls and nothing left in her to manage a career. She woke up one day and could not move. Her own body had betrayed her. She was sent to the Hospital for Joint Diseases in New York.

Nevertheless, she managed to marry my father while still unable to walk. When she became pregnant with me, she recovered just enough to regain the ability to walk and to have more control of her hands. She considered me her miracle child, the one who brought her health and happiness. I continued to be a source of comfort to her throughout my childhood by giving her massages, fetching things she could not reach, opening cans, or carrying objects she could not manage on her own, like Christmas trees, which I would put up and decorate with Alma. I hung curtains, changed light bulbs, nailed pictures on the wall, set the table, and helped with the preparation of dinner. First and foremost, I was my mother's confidante. I listened to her innermost secrets, disappointments, and concerns. Her greatest suffering came from my father's infidelities, and his lack of interest and involvement in the family. Her greatest joy, she repeated to me on many occasions, was being our mother. This added to the estrangement I felt from my father, who did not show much delight in his role as a parent, and to the perception I had of my mother as a victim whose few enjoyments in life came from her children. I saw myself as her solace.

Because I was with her so much, I was privy to conversation and gossip that were meant for adults.

I heard about how the brother of a classmate of mine had killed a gang member in a rumble and about the child of a neighbor of ours being molested and thrown from the roof. There was also the light-skinned black man who thought he was better than anyone else, according to some of the residents of our building. One day, the police came and took him away because he was a suspect in a rape case in Brooklyn. Apparently, he had already served time for such a crime. Dolores, a neighbor from the tenth floor, had always been convinced that there was something strange about the guy.

I also heard my mother's friends complain about the infidelities and stinginess of their husbands. There was a sense of resignation about the role in which the women found themselves. Many seemed to be trapped in relationships due to economic reasons. They just did not have the resources or skills to raise children on their own.

Once, when I was left with a neighbor, I was told to hide because the woman's husband was trying to get into the apartment. Eventually, he got in and began beating her. The woman screamed and cursed and cried. I was hiding underneath a vanity, completely terrified and immobile.

There were two other incidents that gave me a sense of the world being a dangerous place. These incidents occurred outside of the projects and in Manhattan. One day when we were in Chelsea visiting Alma's godmother, Helen, a very polite white man approached me while I was sitting on the front stoop of Helen's building, just below her window. He asked me to help him find a person in the building. I was so proud that he asked me, a six-year-old, to assist him. I entered the building with him and he lured me up to the roof and molested me. Luckily, the kids I had been playing with came looking for me; the man panicked and ran off before he could injure me further.

Another incident occurred on Easter Sunday. We went to visit my grandmother, who lived on 145th Street in Harlem. I was wearing a brand-new coral-colored topper, which was a kind of loose overcoat worn in the 1950s. A group of kids approached Alma and me and began taunting us. One of the kids pulled out a knife and stabbed me in the back. The blade shredded my coat, but it only scratched my skin, because I was prudent enough to have arched my back.

I remember being warned by my mother not to go into an elevator by myself or go to another floor in the building without Alma, which put me on constant alert for possible "bad" men hiding in hallways or staircases. I rarely walked down the stairs; I ran everywhere I went in the building, my heart always pounding furiously. Danger lurked around every corner, I thought.

The objects of my fear were predominantly men. The boogeyman, *el cuco*, was a man, after all. Men were a mysterious group to me. They were not around much and they went off every day to the real world filled with adventure and other men.

Most of the adult figures in my life were women, mothers, teachers, and later, nuns. When fathers came home from work, they were remote and serious; they demanded respect and wielded authority. The kids had to quiet down. Men did not play with the children. Children were to be seen and not heard. The women scurried all around to fetch them food and meet their needs. Once the men got home from work, the women suddenly became different people; they were no longer the relaxed free spirits that they had been throughout the day. They were now docile and quiet.

When there were parties, the men became more human; perhaps it was the *cerveza* or the liquor. They laughed and danced. Men knew about the world. My father, Francisco Manuel Rubal, better known as Manolo, especially seemed to know about everything. He is one of the most knowledgeable and brilliant persons I have ever encountered. He had served in Europe during World War II and had countless stories about many exotic places and extraordinary people. As a child growing up in San Pedro de Macori in the Dominican Republic, he spent countless hours at one of his favorite pastimes—reading history. To this day, there are few people who can match his amazing range and depth of knowledge of world history. He never ceases to amaze me.

Manolo had led the life of *un boemio*, a free spirit who dedicated his time to wine, women, song, politics, art, and tango. He, along with his newly widowed mother, Francisca Espinosa de Rubal, better known as Panchita, and his brother, Miguel, had to flee from the Dominican Republic because it was becoming increasingly dangerous to live within the repressive dictatorship of Rafael Leonidos Trujillo. Manolo had participated in one of the first student protests against Trujillo, and Panchita was concerned about reprisals. My grandfather, Francisco Rubal, a Spaniard and a businessman who had retired from the Spanish navy after the dismantling of *la marina* immediately following the Spanish-American War, had died some years earlier in a questionable "accident." *Don* Rubal had been an outspoken critic of the Trujillo regime. His accident was cloaked in mystery. *Abuela* Panchita was not taking any chances with her sons. She migrated to her native Puerto Rico.

A brilliant student in the Dominican Republic, Manolo found it difficult to adjust to a high school curriculum in English. United States language policy varied throughout Puerto Rican history. When my father arrived in Puerto Rico, high school was conducted in English with Spanish as a mandatory subject. This discouraged him and he dropped out before getting a diploma.

He moved to New York in his early twenties, but without a diploma and lacking English skills, he found only low-skill jobs mostly in big hotels. When he was not working, he was wrapped up in politics and the arts. He was a believer in Marxism and Socialism. He was an advocate for the working man and for equal distribution of wealth. He had grown up under a dictator who was supported by the United States and was therefore firmly opposed to U.S. involvement in Latin America. While a student , he had been exposed to the Nationalist Party and became a proponent of the independence and self-determination of Puerto Rico.

In his spare time, he founded and published an arts magazine called *Sangre Nueva* for the Hispanic population in New York. It featured interviews with noted Hispanic artists of the time, theater and book reviews, and listings of upcoming theatrical and cultural events. The publishing of the magazine ended abruptly when he was drafted into the army during World War II. His inability to test well in English made him a prime candidate for grunt work in the infantry. He cleaned toilets and swept classrooms throughout basic training. A serendipitous incident changed the direction of his life and the role he played in the war. While cleaning a meeting room, he noticed some trigonometry problems that had been left unsolved on a blackboard. He became interested and instead of wiping the board off immediately, he began solving them, as a lark. A superior officer and engineer spotted him. When questioned about his knowledge of higher mathematics, my father explained that he had studied trigonometry and calculus in the Dominican Republic. Recognizing Manolo's usefulness, the commanding officer had him transferred to the artillery division, where he was trained in machinery and served with a team of engineers. In his new position, he saw heavy action in Germany.

Manolo was not around much when I was young. He would leave the apartment before dawn to drive out to Long Island, where he worked as a machinist in the airplane industry. I never saw him in the morning, only when he returned from work. After bathing, changing clothes, eating, and drinking coffee, he was out the door. I never asked where he was going and he never volunteered the information. My mother confided to me later that he was with other women, attending cultural and political events, or with friends. He seemed to inhabit another world.

The time Manolo did spend at home was memorable. There were many smoke-filled Sunday afternoons with Argentine tangos blasting on the hi-fi and the *New York Times*, the *News*, and the *Herald Tribune* spread across the living room. He dominated the apartment when he was around. If the television was on, it was on the program of his choice. He was the sovereign in his own home. I remember my mother timing precisely when she made the evening coffee, because Manolo had to have it immediately after eating the last bite of his dinner. It had to be black, strong, hot, and sweet.

There were family outings, however. My father would drive us into Manhattan past Rockefeller Plaza or Times Square, which at that time was fascinating, with its Pepsi advertisement of a waterfall and a billboard for Camel cigarettes that blew rings of smoke.

When we went to the beach, it was not to Orchard Beach in the Bronx, which he called *la playa de los mojones* (this translates as "turd beach"). We would be on the road by 5:30 a.m. and go to Heather Hills in Montauk, Long Island. It was a two-and-a-half-hour drive, but the beach was truly magnificent.

During these times together there was no real dialogue. He rarely spoke to us directly, and when he did, it was meant more as a lecture or a sermon and we were his audience. He never asked us about our schooling or our interests or concerns. Instead, he spoke through our mother, who was like a middleman and became conveyer of his sentiments.

Manolo did not believe in spending money on "trivialities" like clothing. This was difficult for a self-conscious teenager like myself to grasp. I remember needing a winter coat while in high school. He brought one home from the Salvation Army that was about five times too large for me. He could not understand my dismay because the coat was warm and well-made. What it looked like was not important. On the other hand, when he got tickets to an important event like the Bolshoi Ballet, they were front-row, center seats. Cultural events were not trivialities and money for them was considered money well spent.

My introduction to New York museums was due to my father. These included not only the well-known Metropolitan, the Museum of Modern Art, and the Guggenheim; he also took us to the lesser-known Frick Collection and to his beloved Hispanic Museum across from the Museum of the American Indian on 154th Street and Broadway. I was familiar with Goya, Velazquez, Sorrolla, and El Greco at an early age. My father was very passionate about another great Spaniard—Picasso. His enthusiasm and excitement about the arts and literature were contagious. I remember in high school deciding to read the entire works of Victor Hugo during a summer break. I read *Candide* by Voltaire and the plays of Molière, because he was appalled that only American and English literature was emphasized in the American school system. He claimed that my education would be incomplete with exposure only to literature written in English. I even picked up a book about Einstein because of my father's interest in relativity.

At parties Manolo seemed to always be the center of attention. If he wasn't dancing the tango or reciting poetry, he was debating. The men would often get into heated discussions about politics. This always made me anxious, because I perceived men as unpredictable and could not distinguish between their passion and their aggression. Energetic discussions felt like feuds, which could lead to possible danger. I never saw this happen, but sometimes men stopped speaking to each other for years because of opposing political views. A case in point was a heated discussion about Fidel Castro between my Uncle Guillermo and my dad. A bet was made. Castro had just overthrown Batista and my father claimed that Castro would last for years to come. Guillermo felt that he would be ousted in less than a year. Needless to say, my father won the case of scotch. But things were never the same. There was resentment and bitterness all around.

Although I know better now, men seemed to have it all. Men made the decisions, they owned and drove the cars, they got to choose whom they would marry or have an affair with, and the men got to leave the Bronx. Women could only react to male decisions; they were the ones chosen. Women were trapped—except, that is, those who had education and could be economically independent.

It was many years before I realized that the builders of that safe haven and community of which I was a part were the women. At some point during my childhood, I made the decision never to be dependent on a man; I was never going to be with someone because I could not afford to live without his economic support.

I had my mother as a role model. Despite the hand that she was dealt, she had more control of her life than most of her gender did. Furthermore, her pictures and mementos were testimony to a world more dangerous and exciting than the one on 145th Street and Third Avenue in the Bronx.

Alma

The first memories of my childhood are not of poverty, suffering, abuse, or any of the great evils or images that are usually associated with being brought up in a low-income project in the South Bronx. As a child, in fact, I was living in a world that could be categorized as one of luxury compared to that of many of the Puerto Ricans in the South Bronx, who were living in neighborhoods adjacent to the projects. They lived in deplorable conditions. Little did I know that during my childhood this was as good as it would get. In comparison with many of our cousins and friends who did not live in projects, we were blessed, as we lived in a warm, modern building. Stereotypes of roach-infested tenements with no heat, no hot water, and crumbling walls did not apply to us, at least not while we lived in Patterson Projects. This is not to say that we were not poor; in retrospect, our poverty was not one that is commonly presented in the novels that depict Puerto Ricans. We did not live the life described in Oscar Lewis's book *La Vida* or the type of existence depicted in *Down These Mean Streets*. The by-products of poverty such as crime, violence, and drugs did touch us, but these things never succeeded in over-shadowing the love and caring that surrounded us. Just as Hispanics differ in who they are, poor people also differ in the substantive nature of that poverty. Poverty is often treated as a generic malady without considering how this phenomenon is played out. In essence, people do not experience poverty in the same way. To be economically deprived is not necessarily the worst thing that can happen to a child. The emotional assault and the breaking of a child's spirit, which are often the result of poverty, but not exclusive to being poor, are what really can kill a child. The richness of growing up in a community in which you belong without having to work for acceptance outweighs any lack of money and material possessions.

The residents of Patterson consisted predominantly of intact families with working fathers and mothers who stayed at home and took care of their children. On our floor, for example, we had a bread factory worker, two policemen, a mailman, a truck driver, a mattress factory worker, and my father, who was employed as a tool and die worker in the airplane industry. All had at least two children and were indeed married to the mother of their children. No one on our floor had a drug problem, beat their wives, or had been incarcerated at any time. Furthermore, with the exception of the Clooneys, who were the only white family on our floor, the families were either African American or Puerto Rican.

The projects in the South Bronx were created after World War II to house the returning veterans and their families. The construction of the projects happened to coincide with a large migration of

African Americans from the southern United States and the largest migration during the 1950s of Puerto Ricans to the mainland United States. Not surprisingly, this was the racial composition of our neighbors. Our community was made up predominantly of persons of color with a few scattered white people. As the whites, or *Americanos*, as we referred to them, moved out to whiter areas, the projects became totally black and Puerto Rican.

My most vivid childhood memories are of a neighborhood comprising people who knew your name and who had no problem scolding you if your behavior warranted it, but they were also people who were there if you needed them. In essence, we were a community, and there was a shared sense of responsibility for the well-being of our neighbors. In this way our project was like a village, and it took the interest, love, and caring of everyone in that village to provide me with the many fond memories that I have today.

This sense of community provided a relatively safe haven for us. We were all poor and no one had an edge over the other. This equalization, which resulted in the absence of competition and materialism, allowed us to become engaged in one another's lives. As children, we spent our free time going from home to home and playing with one another's toys, and from this we all learned that poverty is without a doubt the mother of invention. Since no one had a vast number of toys, it became apparent to us that the daily rounds to one another's homes was the way to approach this inadequacy. As we took one or two toys from each home, we would finally end up with a complete set of the necessary toys to play house. The teacup set might belong to one person, while the pretend kitchen might be someone else's, and so on. And to this day, I wonder if the mothers sat around and decided what to get each of us for Christmas. The problem was that the number of kids grew as we made our daily rounds and became somewhat unmanageable for the small apartments. At this point, we were usually asked to leave by the parent and moved our playing out into the hallway or back to our apartment. Because of all the mothers, ours was the one who did not mind having children invade her space and mess up the apartment. Our apartment became the place to hang out, especially once my uncle, Miguel, whom we haven't heard the last of, met Rosalyn, the Jewish woman whom he eventually married. This worked out perfectly for us, because we inherited the toys and clothes of her deceased daughter, Ellen. These were not just any toys; they were not the Woolworth crap that we were accustomed to playing with. One day my father brought home these amazing toys, and we could not believe our eyes. There, in the middle of our living room, stood a real stuffed pony that swung from front to back. It was like riding a real horse, and there were dolls with hair that looked real and books with hand-painted pages with Ellen's name embossed on them; the story of Cinderella had a carriage that would open up to a pumpkin-like shape, and much more. It was like Christmas in July. These toys were like nothing I had ever seen; they were the toys of the rich and we, in the middle of a project in the South Bronx, had inherited this fortune. The excitement was just too much to bear. The next morning while our parents slept, Angie and I took turns getting on the horse. While one rode, the other examined the rest of the treasures. As soon as we heard noise in the hallway outside, we went to the other kids' homes to let them know of our windfall. No need for our caravan of toy-deficient children to go from home to home now. It was party time in our house. However, it soon became tiring when we had to engage in crowd control for turns on the horse. But I must admit that this gave me a sense of power; it was my first and only experience with controlling the means of production and quite frankly my last. But it was a memorable one. This unequal distribution of wealth was great, but as a child it was rather strange. Why did we get all this? It was a peculiar situation, but one that was most enjoyable. Nevertheless, we continued to make the rounds from apartment to apartment. We had no choice. The mothers knew that having all these children at all times in our home was an imposition, so we divided our time among homes, with ours being the final and longest stop. Yes, we would go from one apartment to another without much thought given to whose house we were in.

The apartments were distinguished not by what each looked like or contained but by the smells coming from what was being cooked that day. Dolores's collard greens were a smell that got my attention because it was a scent to which my senses were not accustomed. On the other hand, the smell of the beans that Lydia cooked every day went practically unnoticed, because it resembled that of my home. This is not to say that my mother's beans tasted like Lydia's. Although my mother spent much of her time trying new recipes she had cut from magazines, I have to say that cooking was not her forte. There were a few dishes that she did well, but in general, Puerto Rican cooking was not her strong suit. Actually, cooking in general was not one of her talents. My father, who has never been a great consumer of food, never complained about my mother's cooking, which was interpreted by her as an indication of her great culinary talent, and thus motivated her to provide cooking lessons to the rest of the neighbors. So, all of a sudden, there was this woman with very limited ability in the kitchen who had taken it upon herself to become the Julia Child of the project. She became so confident in her culinary ability that she would substitute ingredients. Ironically, whatever she taught was duplicated and improved by the person learning. One of my father's closest friends, Billie, was an African American woman from South Carolina who lived on the same street as my grandmother in Harlem. Every Thanksgiving we went to Billie's for dinner. She was a great cook. Billie taught my mother how to make Southern fried chicken, which she quickly passed on to our Puerto Rican neighbors. Ironically, everybody's fried chicken was delicious; it was crispy, tasty and golden brown, while my mother's was soggy, white, and just not like everyone else's. One night she decided to make beef stroganoff, a dish that was a deviation from our daily rice and beans or plantains. I remember my father saying to her, *Esto parece carne guisada* ("This looks like beef stew"). My mother responded indignantly by saying that it was not *carne guisada*. When I asked why the meat looked so dark, she said, "Well, it might be the grape juice that I substituted for the red wine." My father looked at me with his same look of disgust that he always had when he came home and was not fed his rice and beans. After working a long day, the last thing that my father desired was to be a guinea pig. Nevertheless, he ate what he was fed, but it became too much to bear when he was expected to like it. When probed about how delicious the meal was, he became upset and responded, "What do you wish for me to tell you, that I like this? All I want is some rice and beans and meat." I could see my mother's disappointment, but quite frankly I was also longing for something familiar and recognizable, something that would not activate my gag reflex. My father's frankness is one of his predominant characteristics. He prides himself on being a man of integrity. Looking back, he was certainly not the person from whom to seek a compliment.

My mother even expanded her talents to other domains. Her *cojones*, her balls in other words, were not confined to the kitchen. One morning she woke up and decided that my hair needed to be cut, and somehow got it into her head that cutting hair was a piece of cake. She sat me on the toilet seat, put a bowl on my head and an apron around my neck and transformed me into the South Bronx version of the Buster Brown boy. All I needed was the dog. For the rest of the day I stared into the mirror in disbelief. The only thing that kept me from crying was that my sister, Angie, whose hair was as curly as mine was straight, had undergone the same procedure, and she looked worse. I might have looked like the Buster Brown kid, but she looked like a poodle. My mother, who was not a stupid woman, must have realized the extent of what she had done, because for the rest of the day she told us how beautiful we looked. I remember her telling Angie that she now looked like Annette Funicello of the Mouseketeers, and she told me that I looked like a cherub from heaven. I don't know how Angie accepted this newfound Disney identity, but I did not buy my mother's comparison of me to a celestial being. How could she tell me that I was a demon one moment, an accusation that she frequently made, and then turn around and tell me that I now looked like a cherub? I might have looked like an angel, but I assure you that after looking at myself in the mirror my thoughts were strongly grounded in hell. And how she convinced the neighbors to let her cut their children's hair is beyond my comprehension, especially after they had seen us, but she did. Everyone got the same haircut regardless of hair texture.

It must be noted that she was before her time. Yes, my mother brought forth the whole idea of the Afro fifteen years before Angela Davis. Kids would enter our home in joy and leave in shock. In school we would look at one another with empathy and knew that we shared a common experience—namely, that we were victims of Carmen's *casa de belleza* (house of beauty), where you were guaranteed a beauty makeover the like of which you would never again experience.

Carmen Bryan de Rubal was not only the self-appointed Julia Child of the ninth floor, she was also everyone's confidant, emergen-

cy doctor, psychologist, party planner, hair dresser, marriage counselor, and translator. The Irish have their priests, the Italians have
their dons, the Jews have their rabbsi, and the people of our projects
had Carmen Bryan de Rubal. She was a multitalent who was sought
by all. My mother was the one who would go with the parents to
register their kids in school because they could not speak English;
she would read prescriptions, write letters, explain bills written in
English, and accompany them to the public health clinic. It would
not be an exaggeration to say that many of the non-English-speaking parents made choices about where their kids went to school,
what doctors they saw, and the community services that they received because of my mother's intervention. This woman with a
high school diploma, who spoke English and Spanish, who had been
John Rockefeller's secretary, served as a translator, and who came
from a family in which her father was a judge educated in Spain, was
quite an unusual person. Furthermore, her extraordinary beauty,
along with the way she talked, the way she carried herself, and the
zeal with which she approached life, was different from the rest of
those around her. Unlike the rest of the Puerto Rican mothers, who
had very little education and had married very young and had children, my mother had graduated from high school, had a career in
Puerto Rico, and later moved to Florida, where she worked as John
Rockefeller's secretary. She had been a career woman who did not
have her first child until the age of thirty-one. She was a woman who
was born to a family that was educated and fairly wealthy. As a child
she had a house in the city of Mayaguez and a weekend and summer
home on a five-hundred-acre farm in Las Marias, in the mountains
of Puerto Rico. I am told that there is currently a school in that
vicinity, named *La Escuela Tomas Bryan* after my grandfather. When
my mother spoke to us of her childhood, she spoke of her great love
for her father, who had died in the river on their farm while trying to save his oldest daughter from being engulfed by a whirlpool.
He saved her, but in the process lost his own life. Images of her
childhood depicted a life of comfort, opulence, and refinement. My
mother's house had a baby grand piano and violins and each child
had a nanny. Her grandmother, our great-grandmother, who was
French, had a special dispensation, a privilege not easily attained by
a woman, to execute parts of the mass in the absence of a priest. Her

sister attended Barnard College, her brother attended City College School of Engineering, her sister Luisa went to Hunter College, and her brother Carlos was an engineer and graduate of the University of Gainesville. Such personal history was not only unusual for someone living in the projects, it was unusual for most citizens of the United States, who at the time consisted of a very small number of persons who had ever attended college. Her ending up in low-income projects was not what anyone would have ever imagined for her, but life has a way of putting detours in one's path. Her detour came in the way of sickness. While living in Florida, she became paralyzed with crippling arthritis that attacked her body with a vengeance few doctors had ever seen. She came to New York for medical treatment and rented a room in my paternal grandmother's apartment in Harlem, where she met my father. He had just returned from World War II. They fell in love, married, and moved to a basement apartment on 17th Street in Manhattan, where Angie was born. As a newborn, Angie had been hospitalized on several occasions for pneumonia, bronchitis, and asthma. My parents were then approached by the hospital social worker, who suggested finding them an apartment in a project because the basement was too humid and too cold and the coal that was burning beside them was affecting Angie's lungs.

Although my mother never complained about where or how she lived, it was obvious that there was something different about her. Nevertheless, she played the hand that she had been dealt, and for the most part accepted her fate the best that she could. However, once in a while I would detect sadness in her that now, as an adult, I can understand. When she spoke of her childhood, she spoke of debutantes, horseback riding on her farm, and her father's progressive ways. He encouraged his daughters to seek an education and seemed to be the nurturer of the family. She had pictures of her many adventures when she was a single woman. She flew planes, shared a house with three women in Miami, and had her share of dating some very exciting men, including a reporter and a pilot. She had even been engaged to a chemist.

These stories were so compelling, and yet I never heard her share them with any of the neighbors. She might have tried to blend into the crowd and knew that this knowledge would only add to her uniqueness among her neighbors. I remember her anger at Dorothy

Clooney, our next-door neighbor, who happened to be Irish and of the opinion that all Puerto Ricans were uneducated and inferior to her. Apparently, my mother had had a conversation with her in which she revealed her feelings. My mother looked at me and said, "You know, Alma, these stupid *Americanos* meet a few Puerto Ricans and make generalizations about us. In Puerto Rico there are many educated people who wouldn't give the Clooneys the time of day. In my family we do not have factory workers living in projects. If they are so superior, what are they doing living in a project, and why does your father give Mr. Clooney a ride to work in the morning because he can't afford a car? She is too stupid to realize that I am somebody." My mother, of course, failed to mention that we owned a jalopy that oftentimes would break down, but in any event her words stayed with me. This conversation has remained with me throughout my life, and my mother's fury became mine. Throughout my life I have encountered countless moments when I would whisper to myself those same words. Those words have been there at times when I have been denied housing or employment or when I have entered the homes of some of my white friends, in particular those of the opposite sex, and their parents first find out that I am Puerto Rican. These words have been particularly comforting for me when people around me have taken upon themselves the task of lecturing to me about particular issues or questioning my abilities. All of a sudden, as if from nowhere, come those words and I find myself thinking, "Hey stupid, you know that I am somebody. Yes, I am somebody and you are too ignorant to even see it." This internal conversation, although helpful in providing me with the mind-set needed to get through some difficult times, also marginalized me. Unintentionally, my mother was agreeing with Dorothy Clooney and telling me that I was different from the other people of the projects. My mother would tell us stories about how the name Bryan was from England and how her mother's name, Arana, was from the Basque region of Spain and that indeed Souffront (from our great-grandmother) was a French name. She wanted us to distinguish ourselves from the Ortizes, the Lopezes, and the Riveras, the names of the other Puerto Ricans in our building. Her stories of her family's accomplishments contributed to my feeling like someone, but these stories also planted the seed that I was different. This sense of belonging to but not really being a part of something has followed me throughout my life and, on occasion, has allowed me the opportunity to have a bird's-eye view of my situation.

To return to my childhood, as we grew up, our play expanded to the streets, where we engaged in skating, bicycling, climbing fences, baseball, stickball, hockey board, checkers, jump rope, double Dutch, Chinese jump rope, hula loops, and many other activities. Like our play in our homes, our toys were shared by all. My first skating experiences were on skates owned by someone else. When there were too many children to share skates,, we would each grab one, take a skate key and expand them to fit us, and ride on one skate. What strikes me about my experience playing in the streets is the vast amount of time that we spent with our peers without any adult supervision, and the vast distances that we covered. Unlike childhood today, where kids are engaged in planned activities and there is always an adult present, we created our own experiences, and we were the kings and queens of our turf. The cardinal rules of play were quite simple. One, you waited your turn; two, you shared your toys; three, if you were using someone's bike or skates, you must abide by the owner's wishes of how long and how far you could use his/her belongings; and lastly, never ever steal anyone's stuff. Any deviation from these rules would make you a target of a beating handed out by your peers, you would be considered an outcast, and no one, but no one, would ever play with you again. Unlike most of the Puerto Rican girls in the neighborhood, who were not allowed to roam the streets, Angie and I were given the freedom to survey our turf. My mother, who decided to start working when I was in the second grade, went from being the neighborhood's problem solver to a working mother, and we went from kids who were always supervised to kids who became street savvy and tough. Lydia, our neighbor and my mother's closest friend in the projects, kept an eye on us when we came home from school, but her supervision was from her apartment while we were in ours. She had instructions to let us go out and play, and we made sure that we took advantage of this. Also, on weekends and during the summers, the streets were ours to roam however we pleased.

My first street fight occurred over racial slurs that were exchanged between myself and two African Americans, a brother and sister. They called me a spic and I countered by calling them niggers, a term that I had heard before and knew would hurt them, but I did not know why. This term or any other racial or ethnic slur was never used in our home, so I assume that it was picked up in the street. In any event, I exchanged a few blows, a few scratches, kicks, and punches, and to my surprise they ran away crying. I fought away my tears, but could feel my face on fire. That evening there was a knock on our door, and my mother answered the door. There stood a tall, thin, light-skinned black woman, who told my mother that I had beaten both of her children. Both children stood there with bruises and scratches on their faces. My mother called me to the door and the two mothers made us promise to never again engage in such interchanges. Although my mother's disapproval of my behavior was apparent, I did dwell on the fact that I was able to kick the ass of two kids at the same time, while a whole mess of black teenagers urged them on to kick the spic's ass. My only regret was that there were few kids outside that afternoon to witness this champion fight. Nevertheless, when I went out the next day, there stood the brother and sister team pointing me out to their friends and telling them of our fight. I stood there waiting to see what they were going to do, but no one moved, so I went on my merry way to look for my friends.

Most of my fights were not with friends but with Angie. We would go to blows for anything, from what television show we wanted to see to who had the greatest amount of soda. In those days soda was a luxury, so when we had the opportunity to share a bottle of Coke, we would have fights over the amount, which was difficult to determine in a household whose glassware came in an array of jelly jars that all varied in size. One day Angie and I got into such a rage that our fists were not enough, and we began to throw things at each other. We picked up anything that was available—ashtrays, lamps, figurines, whatever could serve as a projectile weapon. When there was nothing left to throw, we sat there facing each other, crying and yelling at each other. Then reality seeped in: All of those broken objects needed to be repaired before our parents came home or our heads would be the next items to be cracked in half. Angie and I quickly got glue and glued every item together. Any crack on any item was situated in a way that one could not see it. This deception was temporary, for when my mother cleaned the house on Saturday, she realized that something was not right. The first indication was a hideous-looking ashtray of a Chinese woman that was found to have a crack in it. When she inquired, we kind of looked at one another and shrugged our shoulders. We had no idea how that crack had appeared, and my mother bought our story. However, a few minutes later when she continued her dusting, she found that the lamp's leg fell off and its apparent damage was revealed. By this time my mother realized what had happened and warned us of the consequences of fighting. To our surprise, she left it at that.

As we got older, technology entered our world and impacted our lives in ways that we never could have imagined. For many years no one in our building had a phone, until my parents decided that this would be a worthy asset to our household. My mother said that she had decided to have a phone installed because she was usually alone with Angie and me and we both suffered from chronic asthma. In case of an emergency, she could have easy access to a phone. Our apartment became the building's center of communication. People came to us to receive and to make calls, and Angie and I unwittingly became the pony express of our building. When calls were received, we would run to the apartment of the person awaiting a phone call and alert them to come in a hurry. When long distance calls were received, entire families would come to speak to their relatives. Since most of the people in the projects at the time had a limited experience with telephones, it was not uncommon for people to scream unnecessarily or to speak into the hearing part of the phone rather than the receiver. We became well informed on some very personal details of many of our neighbor's lives. We knew when our neighbors owed money, did not go to work, were having guests over, or when there was a death or birth in their extended families.

As time went on, television became more and more popular. Since we were one of the first families to have a television in our building, I can remember parents coming to our home to survey this new phenomenon and asking questions about its cost and how it worked. Soon everyone had a television, and this new invention became progressively more important in our lives, as it went from an occasional thing to watch to the electronic babysitter, news provider, and all-around focus of our lives. Little did we know then that we would become victims of the images depicted by the seemingly benign shows that we viewed every week.

As a child, shows like *Father Knows Best, Donna Reed, Ozzie and Harriet,* and *Leave It to Beaver* made me wonder why we did not live in split-level homes with white picket fences. I remember looking out the window of my room and trying to find a star to wish on every night. My wish was to live in such a home. The mother who stayed home and the father who came home from work in a suit and said, "Hello, dear. I'm home," was foreign to me. No one in my neighborhood went to work in a suit, and no one returned home after a long day's work with the cheerfulness and energy depicted in any of those shows. Fathers arrived from their jobs dirty and smelling like sweat or chemicals. A mother who never screamed or hit her kids and who always looked good was not part of my life. A home with a father who rarely shared any time with his family, a sick, depressed mother who lived in the past with very little hope for the future—this is what showed when the curtain went up in my household. The tube depicted the Anderson family while I was stuck living in the Addams family.

These shows were dangerous to kids of color because of the absence of any brown faces and the interpretations that could be made, especially by those kids of color who were living in poverty. For the poor white kid, the message was that maybe with hard work and discipline you could make it. After all, there were people like you who had made it. The poor white kid might have an uncle or aunt that lived a different existence, but in the fifties the chances of a poor black or Hispanic kid having a wealthy family member were slim. In fact, we were the ones who were living good compared with our families and friends in tenements. For the poor white kid, the hope was slim but there might be a light at the end of the tunnel. However, for the black or Hispanic child, the message was that there was no light, and there was probably no tunnel, either. There was only a long, long road that led back to where you were, stuck in the projects and poor. Furthermore, the isolation and segregation of the public housing often resulted in false assumptions and dangerous interpretations made by children who looked at television without knowing anything outside of their immediate surroundings. If the only white people you know are those on television, then the assumption becomes that all white people are like those on the tube. It follows that if the parents in these shows provided their families with the comfort that was seen on television, why can't yours? And why is it that only white people are successful? These images quickly transform that father who was your knight in shining armor into Sancho Panza, the incompetent fool. The negative internalization of these images turns into a desire to be like those persons on the screen and to fantasize about a blonde blue-eyed me, an impeccable home, parents who spoke proper English, and a mother and father who were not worn down by the everyday drudgery resulting from poverty and racism. These thoughts occupied too much space in my young mind, and as a result questions were formed, questions asking why life was the way it was, but the answers I received, when answers were given, just did not suffice.

While the children played in each other's homes and on the street and entertained themselves by looking at television, the parents formed ties with one another that lasted a lifetime. Lydia, my mother's closest friend, for example, would visit every night after dinner, because she loved my father's strong *criollo* (Puerto Rican coffee) and would indulge and take the opportunity to talk with my mother. Other neighbors would stop by as well, just to talk and see how we were doing, or to borrow sugar or salt or any other item that they might need.

As the week drew closer to payday and people's cash flow became less and less, it was not unusual for people to make the rounds to see who had some change to spare. When my mother got bored or needed money, she too would make the rounds. I remember neighbors trying to collect enough money for subway tokens to get to work. Our neighbors were very charitable with one another. If they had it and you needed it, it was yours. This willingness to help one another was evident when people died. I remember people from the building knocking at the door and asking for contributions because their spouse or child had died and they needed money for the burial. Everyone would open their doors and contribute some change. The most memorable ways in which adults celebrated their friendships were in the parties that were given in their homes. A child's baptism, birthday, communion, or confirmation was an excuse for a celebration. The parties started in the afternoon for the children, and by nightfall they had become adult parties. Each person came dressed in his or her Sunday best, and everyone contributed something to the event. Women in high heels and dresses with glitter and men in suits knocked at the door and joined in the celebration, with the late-comers spilling into the building hall. After hours of drinking and dancing, the survivors would now take turns telling jokes in Spanish, singing, playing a guitar, arguing politics, and finally reciting poetry. Oftentimes, a nearby apartment was used to cook the food because the apartments were too small to simultaneously cook and party, re-sulting in some of the women having their own personal mini-party while they cooked. No one would ever think of calling the police to complain about the noise, and no one would ever be offended if they were not personally invited. A party meant everyone was in-cluded. No need for formal invitations or RSVPs. News spread like wildfire, and that meant that everyone was considered invited. The informality of those relationships is the one aspect of my life that I never again experienced once we moved out of the projects. The manner in which people interacted and allowed people to engage in their lives was very much like the ways these same people behaved in their small towns, regardless of whether the town was in Machem, Georgia; Durham, South Carolina; or Cayey, Puerto Rico. In cases like this, poverty was like lemons that produce a sweet and delicious lemonade, and it is such memories that keep childhood alive within me, even at age fifty. This is not to say that all was good and that play and parties were the major aspects that encompassed my life, but these memories allow me to extract the good from what at times was a childhood of great sadness, sickness, and fear.

Chapter Two

Early Education
Nuns with Bad Habits

Angie

I never attended preschool and missed most of kindergarten. My mother and my sister and I spent half a year in Puerto Rico prior to my entrance into kindergarten. In those days, many Puerto Rican parents took their asthmatic children to the island in an attempt at a cure. They reasoned that the warm weather would be beneficial.

My asthma had been particularly bad the previous year, and the trip proved beneficial. I did not have an attack for several years following the trip. However, the time we spent in Puerto Rico cut into the time I should have been in school. I arrived sometime in early February, having missed almost half of the academic year.

The adjustment to a cold, dark, and dreary New York after a relaxed, sunny, and beautiful island was very traumatic. And to further complicate matters, when I returned I could not speak English. The time away had eliminated the little English I knew. It was traumatic to be left by my mother in an unfamiliar classroom with strangers with whom I could not communicate. There was no slow transition. My mother was not allowed near the classroom. I remember crying most of the first week in school.

My mother, who had a good command of both English and Spanish, made a major educational decision that was to affect the rest of my schooling. She resolved to have me learn English as soon as possible so that I could survive in school. From then on, mom spoke to Alma and me mostly in English. This became a sore point with my father, who was furious that the language of our heritage was being replaced by the language of the imperialistic Yankee. Because he did not spend much time at home, English became the predominant language of communication at home.

I survived that semester by spending time under my mother's tutelage. I somehow managed to learn English and soon found myself immersed in the normal activities of a kindergarten student. I was promoted to the first grade at P.S. 18 in the Bronx. I think I was a fairly average student. I do not remember grades, but the fear of school subsided and was replaced with a love of learning and doing many new things, such as finger painting, coloring, learning the alphabet, and numbers.

During that time, I was introduced to ballet. I attended free classes at the local community center. I took to ballet immediately. I remember being chosen as the lead dancer in the dance recital, which was performed to Tchaikovsky's *Waltz of the Flowers*. The classes were not continued at the community center after that year, but the dance teacher offered to give me a scholarship. She saw promise in my abilities and wanted to encourage my love of ballet. Unfortunately, her dance studio was on the opposite side of the Bronx. It was very difficult to get there by public transportation, and my father could not arrange to take me on Saturdays. I went once or twice and was very disappointed that I had to stop dancing.

My second grade year was interrupted by an emergency appendectomy. I spent several weeks in the hospital and more weeks in recovery at home. While in the hospital, the children in the pediatric ward were provided with some workbooks donated by the Board of Education and distributed by a teacher. I remember happily and diligently finishing a book at one sitting. The teacher was surprised but concerned that I was going too fast and she would run out of workbooks. The time engaged with schoolwork offered me a refuge from the loneliness and boredom of the hospital.

Again, I missed about half of the school year and again my mother stepped in and extended what I had learned in the first and second grades when I returned home. She did a competent enough job that I was able to keep up with the other students in third grade. Ballet was out of the question, because it would interfere with the healing of the appendix scar, according to the surgeon.

The third grade was an important grade for me, and my mother again played a pivotal role. She had been concerned about the quality of education in our local public school, and when a teacher in the school was stabbed by a sixth grader, she decided to enroll Alma and me in the parish school, St. Rita's. In exchange for our education, mom did office work for the principal.

My admittance into Catholic school represents the time that I associate with the beginning of what I consider the most important part of my formal education—my spiritual development. The contents of the religious instruction I received, such as the notions of evil versus good, heaven and hell, and the nature of God, are not topics formally discussed in public education.

This is the time that I began to think constantly about the meaning of life and my life's purpose. Entering Catholic school also reactivated my fears, not just of this world around me, but also of hell.

Religion and Spirituality

I cannot recall a time that I was not aware of an inner life and being concerned about the meaning of life and my life's purpose. I remember looking at the sky around the age of five or six and wondering why I was sent here. I have always felt that there was something greater than myself, something greater than my body and mind. There has always been a longing for another realm, another home that I know deep down exists somewhere else. I remember not wanting to wake up mornings because I had dreams of speeding through the galaxies among the stars, and the thought of returning to earth was repugnant. At a very young age, I felt that I was part of a grand design in which I had a role—a minor part, but one, nevertheless. The pursuit for meaning has been an unwavering theme in my life. It led me to embrace religion and spirituality at an early age and to becoming an interfaith minister as an adult. Both spirituality and religion have played such an important part in my life that I cannot speak about my educational development without some discussion of them.

Ironically, I was born to an agnostic mother and an atheist father who had an intense antipathy toward the Catholic Church. As fate would have it, I was placed in Catholic school in the third grade. Prior to that, I had attended a local public school.

My father was not happy about the arrangement, but he acquiesced because my mother felt we would get a better education in

Catholic school. He did not get involved much in our day-to-day lives—the logistics associated with the education of his daughters fell to my mother. This did not prevent him from criticizing the Church whenever the opportunity presented itself. He turned to history to make his points against the Church. He passionately delineated the horrors of the Inquisition and the abuse of power connected with indulgences and other methods of buying oneself into so-called "heaven." He relished describing corrupt cardinals and unethical popes; the trial of Galileo; the Church's lack of moral action against slavery and fascism; and the accumulated wealth of the Vatican, which could be used to help people in a true Christian way. God did not escape his antagonism. No one had proven the existence of God, and even if they could, how would you explain a deity who did nothing about all the suffering and injustice in the world?

It was very difficult to be a devout Catholic under these circumstances, but I persisted and even aspired to be a nun for quite some time. There were several possible reasons for this. One was that it was a kind of childhood rebellion. After all, how do you rebel against an atheist father, except by going in the opposite direction and becoming a nun? This would have been very embarrassing for my father.

But the truth is that the Church, and more precisely, the belief in an afterlife where one can count on divine justice to reward the good people, was very comforting to me. Besides, my dad did not fit my picture of a good parent or spouse and he was not at home much, so his opinion did not influence me as much as the idea of the ultimate dad in the sky—*Papa Dios*—the father to top all fathers. *Papa Dios* became the only adult figure who was trustworthy and on whom I could rely.

I had trust in God, despite the fear and religious confusion generated by the Catholic school nuns. The first time I saw my third grade teacher, Sister Rose Dominic, I thought she was from a different planet. I had never seen such strange clothing. Was the habit part of her anatomy? Was she male or female? It was difficult to tell. Why was she called sister? I was told that she was the bride of Christ. Later, I found out that Christ had a lot of brides. All the nuns in the school were his brides. They all had wedding rings and lived under one roof. Christ had a kind of harem happening in the Bronx.

But they were all pure. They had taken vows of chastity, poverty, and obedience.

I spent a great deal of my youth very confused about God. The concept of the Trinity was explained to me by reference to a three-leaf clover: one stem and three leaves, one God with three parts. First, there was a young son who died on the cross, suffered for us, and had a lot of brides. Also, He was the only God who had a mother—the Virgin Mary. Then there was the Holy Ghost. I never could get what the job of the Holy Ghost was, except that he got the Virgin Mary pregnant with Jesus. He was sort of the invisible God. He came down on Pentecost Sunday and caused the disciples to speak in different tongues. Other than this, he was not a significant player in this trio.

Then there was God the father, who had a beard and was old. He was Jesus Christ's father, but he was not the Virgin Mary's spouse; that was St. Joseph. God the father was the "head" God who made the major decisions such as whether or not to throw you in hell for all eternity if you were bad. God the father was all-just, all-good, all-powerful, all-knowing, and all-loving. His biggest drawback was that he had a temper and could send floods, pestilence, boils, and all sorts of bad things your way if he chose to. From my limited perspective, he seemed to be impulsive and arbitrary. But then, we were too stupid to understand his decisions. We were also evil. We came into this world with original sin, so we deserved to suffer. We had to have faith and trust that what God the father did was for our own good. I remember spending time with a little girl my age who had leukemia. My mother explained that she was dying. I could not understand why God would let this happen. It was difficult to comprehend how this could possibly be good. I was frightened that he would decide to make me sick too.

But God was always there to listen. We could pray to God and ask him for all sorts of things, including miracles. We could even make bargains with him. I remember my mother took care of two sisters approximately my age, and both of them had hair so long that it fell to their feet. Apparently, the mother had made a vow, *una promesa*, not to cut her daughters' hair for fourteen years if God helped her with her husband. The daughters were having a tough time dragging all this hair around. It was a major event to comb and wash.

But a promise was a promise! Likewise, a neighbor wore only black, gray, or violet colors for many years because of a similar *promesa* made to God.

Besides promises and prayers, God was responsive to gifts. He especially liked candles, rosaries, and flowers. Saints liked these things as well. Saints were part of an inner circle in heaven. They had direct access to God and could intercede on your behalf. Many saints were like doctors who selected specialties. San Lazarus was the saint of lost causes. San Antonio specialized in getting you a husband. The tradition was to invert a statue of San Antonio and keep him on his head until he got you a husband. St. Christopher was for traveling and cars. Many of the apartments in the projects had pictures or statues of Jesus Christ, the Virgin Mary, or a saint draped with a rosary, a bouquet of plastic flowers in front of it, or dried palm leaves from Palm Sunday.

A word about Mary…There were a lot of Virgin Marys. There was *La Virgen de la Guadeloupe, La Virgen del Carmen*, the Virgin of Lourdes, and one in Fatima. She was the same person, but she would drop by at different times, in different countries with different clothes, speaking different languages. You had a choice of Marys to whom you could pray.

When my juvenile mind was not thinking of God as the Monty Hall of the Let's Make a Deal in the Sky, I imagined God as a magnificent Certified Public Accountant, the ultimate CPA. He was The Accountant who kept the books for the human race. Each one of us had a balance sheet that God was constantly updating. To be a good Catholic, one had to understand mathematics and basic accounting. The balance sheet was constantly changing with the notation of good deeds or sins. It was complicated because all actions had numerical values. Sins carried different negative weights. Sins that were not very bad were called venial sins, and they carried less negative valences. The worst sins, the mortal sins that could land you in the fires of hell for all eternity, bore the most potent negative values. Commit a lot of mortal sins and you were doomed forever.

Good deeds, sacrifices, and prayers were rendered positive values. For example, in confession a mortal sin might be atoned with the saying of a rosary. A venial sin could be erased with three Hail Marys (a relatively short prayer) or one Apostle's Creed (a longer prayer). It became even more complicated when you added, let's say, 2,000 plenary indulgences or 300 secondary indulgences into the equation. An indulgence, which is a remission of punishment for sins, could surely change the "bottom line." One minute you could be in the red and the next you were in the black.

The final tabulation on the bottom line was extremely important. If you were deeply in the red you could end up in hell. However, being in the black did not guarantee a ticket to heaven. You might have to spend a while in purgatory to cleanse a few sins. Purgatory was like a holding pen or an extra wash cycle. You did your time to clean up those last few stains on your soul. Seldom did people go directly to heaven. Most had to have that final rinse.

I spent most of my youth trying to find out the numerical values connected with behavior. Was there a formula for staying in the black? How much could I push the envelope and still make the cut for heaven? How many points should I bank in case of a moral slipup?

The nuns told us repeatedly that not going to church on Sunday was a mortal sin. I will never forget an exchange I had with a nun in front of my fourth grade class. I asked her if murder was a mortal sin. She said that it could be. What if I murdered someone on Friday, confessed my sin on Saturday, went to church on Sunday and died on Monday? Would I go to hell? "No," she answered. And what if I did no wrong prior to Sunday but decided to skip Sunday mass and was hit by a bus on Monday? Would I go to hell? "Yes!" was her answer. I could not understand an accounting system that would consider going to church more important than the sanctity of a human life. I kept questioning the justice of this. As I persisted, I was met with impatience and anger. I was told that it was a question of faith.

The fourth grade was pivotal for me; I learned that asking too many questions in school was not a good idea, if I wanted the approval and reinforcement of my teacher. After several exchanges about unbaptized babies going to "limbo" and non-Catholics being damned because they were not in the one and only true religion, I became conscious of the underlying message, which was that to be a good girl was to not question the wisdom of my superiors. I needed to develop faith if I had any chance of going to heaven. I kept my mouth shut. I chose salvation and approval over understanding and logic.

I definitely wanted to avoid the fires of hell, so I prayed and tried to be good. However, I did not want to just avoid hell, I aspired to the best in heaven. The nuns spoke frequently about praying for a "higher place" in heaven. Apparently, just as on earth, heaven had good neighborhoods and bad neighborhoods. I decided that I wanted prime beachfront with a pool and a deck; I wanted the works. I did not want to go the route of public housing in heaven. Being good was unquestionably associated with material rewards. What I did not have on earth, I aspired to in heaven.

Prayer and good works were not the only means to my goal. Making little sacrifices like St. Therese of Lisieux, the Little Flower, was the way to go. During Lent, we were encouraged to give up candy or to stop seeing a favorite television show as a sacrifice to God. I decided not to limit my sacrifices to the Lenten season. Martyrs made the ultimate sacrifices. They were eaten by lions rather than renounce their faith.

Somehow, the notion of suffering as being noble or good took root in my consciousness. Little did I realize that in life you do not have to go out of your way to find ways to suffer. Life will provide you with numerous opportunities. This I would learn later. Unfortunately, I often opted to suffer by forgoing pleasure.

I recall shopping for a much needed winter coat with my mother. I selected the ugliest coat as a sacrifice to God. I reasoned that vanity was a sin, which meant that looking ugly was probably a good thing. I stopped looking at myself in the mirror for a few years in the name of not being vain. In another incident, in order to achieve humility, I purposely failed an exam because I was deriving too much pleasure from getting straight As. Boy, was I accumulating good points! It was like the gold stars the nuns would glue on the back of the holy pictures when we were good. I certainly had my large collection. But I often worried about the sin of pride. I was becoming too proud of accumulating so many points!

The closest I got to martyrdom was my refusal to renounce my faith to my atheist and heathen father. It was a tremendous source of pride for him to say that he had never been baptized. At one point, after learning that baptism could be performed without a priest,

Alma and I baptized my father when he was asleep. At least now he had some chance of avoiding the eternal fires of hell.

Just as the martyrs did, I would hold fast to my beliefs even in the face of pressure. My father's arguments about the Catholic Church did not affect me. I would not budge about going to church on Sunday. No inducement would sway me from moral incorrectness. Any plans for the family on weekends had to include Sunday mass for Angie.

A significant incident occurred in the third grade, which reinforced my feeling that to be spiritual meant sacrifice. In this case, I gave up being liked by fellow classmates.

Our teacher, Sister Rose Dominic, left the classroom and told the class that we were not allowed to talk. Nevertheless, several students spoke in her absence. When she returned, she asked the students to stand up if they had disregarded her orders. Those who stood were given punishment assignments. Unfortunately, the incident did not end there. She addressed the rest of the class and said that these students were disobedient, but at least they were not liars. She knew that there were some among us who had talked and not stood up. These students were in grave danger of losing their souls. She also knew that there were those in the group who knew who these liars were, and it was our duty to tell her their names. This way, she could help root out their wickedness. If we did not tell, we were just as guilty as they were. I remember shaking like a leaf and feeling my heart pound as if it would leap out of my chest. Looking back now, it was quite a decision for an eight-year-old. I raised my hand and told on my classmates. I was called a tattletale.

Thus, being a martyr also meant being picked on or even thrashed by my fellow students. I was the kid you loved to hate or the teacher's pet throughout most of my education. Because I was always prepared for class and I always knew my catechism, I was often given the assignment to go from row to row and ask my fellow students catechism questions. I always reported anyone who could not give me the correct answers. I took my job seriously because if a student did not know their catechism they would be susceptible to losing their faith. I felt that I was doing the right thing. I was often threatened and on a few occasions I was actually hit because I told. I remained stoic and reasoned I was being a martyr for Christ.

During sixth and seventh grades, I spent many of my afternoons after school doing volunteer work at a local senior citizens' home run by the Little Sisters of the Poor. I cleaned bathrooms and fed, washed, and cared for residents. Much later, when I turned away from organized religion, I still felt the calling to serve and derived rewards from helping others. In high school, I became a Red Cross candy striper in a hospital and a volunteer for the Lighthouse for the Blind, serving meals, reading books to them, and performing tutorial duties. Ironically, the seeds of serving others were planted in an attempt to help myself hoard good deeds.

The conviction of the existence of some kind of divine accounting resulted in a rather pessimistic view of life for a child. Because I thought of life as a balance sheet in a ledger, I remember thinking whenever I was having a good time that sooner or later I would have to pay back for this happiness. If I expressed contentment, God would notice and think, "Oops, that is too much happiness there. I'll have to balance that." Behind every good thing in life was an eventual payback. I was always waiting for the other shoe to drop. In order to somehow forestall or avoid this, I had to obscure myself. I felt like the student who just wants to blend in—not be a superstar or a student in trouble, but one who keeps their mouth shut and does not bring any notice to themselves. God had so many people to take care of, perhaps if I remained camouflaged or quiet or sad, he would forget to lower the boom on me. Rather than be happy for the good things I had, I would be happy that the bad things were not worse. The emphasis was more on the bad and the possibility that it could get worse.

A discussion of my spiritual evolvement would be incomplete without mentioning that as a child I made the ridiculous assumption that there was one group of people who had the inside track concerning Catholicism. I was convinced that to be a successful Catholic you had to be Irish. All the nuns who ever taught me were Irish. The parish priests were all Irish. The monsignor was Irish. St. Patrick's Day was a big deal at our school. Girls were required to wear green ribbons in their hair. I was taught to do the Irish jig in the fourth grade and to sing Ireland's national anthem in the fifth grade. I remember wanting to change my name to Patricia and even taking on that name when I played dolls with friends. The only excuse I can give was my naïveté, which did not stop there but extended to other groups as well. For example, I had no idea that there were any Jews in New York City. I knew Jesus had been a Jew but I thought they were in Jerusalem, Galilee, or Bethlehem. When my Uncle Miguel married Aunt Rosalind, I thought she was the most exotic person I had ever met. The Bronx projects were not exactly a microcosm of the world.

Despite these incidents, I must state that I got many wonderful things from Catholic school. Most of the successful Puerto Ricans of my generation attended Catholic school. It provided the best education around from a very dedicated group of teachers. You learned whether you wanted to or not. It was sometimes beaten into you. Corporal punishment and fear were the common motivators, but the alternative—a dangerous, indifferent, and inconsistent public school education—was far worse. I have never heard of a student graduating from a Catholic school who was not able to read or write. Nuns never hesitated in holding students back if they felt they were not ready to advance to the next level. If students were unwilling to learn, they could be dismissed.

But few students were dismissed, in my experience. Topics were reviewed relentlessly until the entire class understood. I have many memories of waiting patiently until a few slower students were able to grasp a mathematical concept or operation. It did not seem odd to wait until the entire class got it, even though it was boring and embarrassing to see students humiliated before their classmates.

Much of my ability to be disciplined and organized came from Catholic school. Listening skills, note taking, and attention to details such as headings, margins, and penmanship were also stressed. I learned cursive writing in the third grade utilizing a fountain pen, which I filled from an inkwell kept on the corner of my desk. We practiced writing by drawing circles to records that played on a phonograph. I had what seemed a permanent ink spot on my middle finger for years. Grades were given for penmanship. Homework assignments, including math, could not have any erasures. It became common practice to use scrap paper before transferring the work to the final paper. Desks were checked for neatness and orderliness. Orderliness was a key element in our lives. We left the room in a certain order; we put our coats away in another. Every day began with a prayer and the Pledge of Allegiance. There seemed to be rituals and rules for everything. In some ways it was very comforting to have such structure and consistency.

We were expected to treat adults with the utmost respect. You addressed a nun as "Sister." "Yes, Sister." "No, Sister." Any deviation from this meant corporal punishment or dismissal. When a nun spoke, you learned to listen carefully. Instructions were to be followed quickly and to the last detail.

School was serious business. The atmosphere was tense and without humor. I was so petrified of being hit or humiliated that I would vomit each morning before I went to school in the early years. My mother never caught on, because I would lock myself in the bathroom each morning.

Respect for books was instilled in the students, and we had the responsibility to keep them covered and as clean as they were when we received them. This meant no underlining or writing in books, necessitating the need for good note-taking skills. Long homework assignments, which had to be signed by parents and checked daily, were part of the routine, as well as frequent tests and quizzes.

With regard to my spiritual life, perhaps the most important contributions to it were the inner states that I experienced when in church, benediction, or on spiritual retreats. I often felt a connection to something deep within me. At other times there were indescribable pangs of love, peace, and joy. Time seemed to stand still.

Also of major significance was the opportunity to meet individuals who were very rare and beautiful. There were two nuns whom I will never forget. They glowed. Their eyes were filled with light and bliss. They were always busy, but they had an inner stillness. They seemed to love everyone, but they were detached at the same time. They were tough teachers without being stern or cruel. They never had favorites or teacher's pets. I admired them and when I thought of becoming a nun, it was to this idea that I aspired.

What changed it all for me? When did I renounce organized religion? First was my experience in Puerto Rico. Being a serious and stern Catholic was the exception rather than the rule in Puerto Rico. The Catholic school that I attended on the island was run by a different order; the Franciscans instead of the Dominicans. Some of these nuns were Hispanic. They were women, not sexless, indefinable beings. They wore sandals. You could see their feet and see them sweat. They seemed more human. They moved their hips and laughed at risqué jokes. They were more relaxed about adolescence and saw nothing wrong with girls wearing makeup. They saw nothing wrong with dating. They laughed a lot. Learning was fun and more relaxed. There was less competition and more cooperative learning. There was more emphasis on a God who loved rather than on a God who punished. Puerto Rican Catholicism is stamped with a flavor of Santerismo. Good Catholics mixed religious traditions with Yoruba rituals. Holy water was used with herbs and potions to ward off evil and put a spell on an enemy.

Another major shift occurred in tenth grade. When we returned from Puerto Rico, I attended a local New York City public high school, because we could not afford private school. My closest friends were not Catholic—three atheists, one Baptist, and two Jews. We spent numerous hours together.

They often walked me to church after school, where I made a visit every day. I was bombarded with questions that made me think. Did I think of Jews as killers of Christ? My Jewish friends told of cruel epithets being hurled at them by Christians. The atheists echoed many of the arguments my father presented, but coming from my peers these arguments put me on alert. I was challenged to give rationales for my beliefs. I was also introduced to literature that opened a new world to me. A library book on psychology had been confiscated from me by one of my Catholic teachers in grammar school because it was on the Index, a list of books that the Church banned for Catholics. Now I was free to read whatever I wanted.

One weekend, I read all of Albert Camus's works. I never went back to church again. I decided to become an existentialist! I read Kierkegaard, Sartre, Kant. To be virtuous with no thought of reward, because there was probably no God, and if there was one, he was indifferent to us—this stopped me cold. To do good because it contributed to the human race resonated in my heart. To act in an unselfish and moral way because I would be part of the creation of an ever-evolving definition of man seized and excited me.

I spent several years as an agnostic and a seeker. I became open to other spiritual traditions and explored other points of view in an attempt to develop my own code of ethical behavior, not one that was given to me.

During that period, I did not acknowledge the longing in my heart for the soul connection that I had experienced at church and in quiet moments at spiritual retreats. It was not until many years later, when I became involved with biofeedback and experimented with alpha states of consciousness, that I once again began to touch those sacred places within myself.

I sought out and found many spiritual paths, such as Unity Services, the Course on Miracles, DMA, Siddha Yoga. All these things led me eventually to being an Interfaith minister and Essence trainer.

Alma

My first experience in school consisted of kindergarten in P.S. 18. It was a modern school that had most likely been built to accommodate the population from the surrounding projects. Miss Barrett, a middle-aged, gray-haired woman, was my teacher. She was everything that a kindergarten teacher should be: warm, enthusiastic, kind, patient, and playful. Our half-day classes were packed with painting, singing, storytelling, and a diversity of other activities, which we all enjoyed. The class, which consisted of ethnically, racially, and culturally diverse students, responded to Miss Barrett as if she were our mother. We cried on her lap in times of despair, hugged her in moments of joy, and disliked her for stopping us from doing things that we saw no wrong in. In an instant, my very small universe was transformed from one consisting of my mother, father, sister, and neighbors to one that now included Miss Barrett and my new kindergarten friends.

My first day in kindergarten was uneventful. My mother had prepared me for this day. She let me know how lucky I was to be going to school and she told me about all the fun that I was going to have. To my surprise, not all of the kids were as prepared as I was for this challenge. On that first day, children were crying and clinging to their parents in desperation. They did not want to be left in a place where they did not understand where they were or why they were there. I remember consoling a little girl who later became a good friend of mine.

In the first grade, I was sent to St. Rita's. Compared with P.S. 18, St. Rita's was old and literally falling apart. In the winter, the wind would creep through the loose, dilapidated windows. We all wore sweaters to keep warm, and there were even times when we were allowed to wear our jackets in class because the school was as cold as an icebox. The nun would sometimes have to bang on the steam pipe so that the school custodian would turn up the heat, or she would send him a note requesting him to please warm up the place. The electricity would also go off at times and not come back on for several minutes. On numerous occasions, it went out for long periods of time. Furthermore, the only working bathroom was in the basement and sometimes it was out of order, and never was there any warm running water. In contrast to the decaying infrastructure of this institution, the school's administration was solid, orderly, and efficient. Sister Eugene was a short, elderly woman who ran the school with the precision of a maximum security prison.

My most memorable recollections of St. Rita's are the bazaars, the plays, and the activities that were thought up to raise money for the school. These activities brought the community together, with parents contributing in one way or another to the given function. This was our school and we were part of its existence. If the school was in danger of economic bankruptcy, it was our responsibility to help keep it from ruin.

Preparation for our plays required practicing our parts until our moves were done with the precision of a Marine Corps platoon, regardless of age or grade. This regimentation was also part of our academic repertoire. It was not uncommon for one of our teachers to throw a book at us if we were talking when we were not supposed to, which was more likely than not the case. Such techniques as taking the boys by the tie and slapping their faces until they were beet red or grabbing girls' ponytails and flinging them from one side of the room to the other for not paying attention were commonly employed in the name of education. If you were unlucky enough to have a nun who was short-tempered, you might even get your knuckles rapped with a ruler or with the leg of a chair for not knowing an answer or for having dirty fingernails. Needless to say, there was great order and silence throughout the school.

The nuns differed in their ability to teach. My experiences ranged from having a nun such as my first grade teacher, Sister Thomas Aquinas, who was a master teacher and inspired and instilled in her students a love of learning, to having some nuns who were mentally and emotionally incapable of teaching children. The nun who taught second grade, Sister Francis Marie, fell into the latter category. She lacked all virtue and had no ability to work effectively with young people. This fat, blue-eyed, freckled, red-faced beast used intimidation as an approach to teach us. Her techniques were similar to that of a drill sergeant. Those students who did not understand or could not keep up with her pace would suffer her wrath. Another nun I had was Sister Alexis. She was an elderly woman who should have retired but who was still teaching. She would fall asleep while talking to the class. We were so browbeaten by our past teachers that we just sat there in silence and observed her sleeping. Although we would usually grin and laugh silently without uttering a word, this silence would come to an end when her sleeping episodes were lengthy. A prolonged sleep would result in an escalation of noise. As we talked to one another, we had one eye on our dear Sister so that we could freeze whatever we were doing before her eyes opened completely. One day we missed a portion of our lunch break because she was asleep. Luckily, one of the other nuns passed our class and saw us sitting there. She quickly awakened Sister Alexis and we were dismissed.

While nuns differed in abilities and approaches, they all expected us to learn. There were no excuses for being inattentive or refusing to participate in the act of learning. Those who did not live up to this expectation would be severely dealt with and ultimately asked to leave the school.

Religion and Spirituality

With regard to religion, it was something that I did rather than something that I felt. The rote memorization of the catechism without knowing or understanding what I was expected to repeat at a moment's notice was undoubtedly the wrong approach to use on a young child on her journey to becoming a spiritual being. Moreover, my young age and the complexity of the subject matter contributed to the inappropriateness and absurdity of such a task. The abstractness of the concepts of God, sin, good, and evil taught to a young child in a manner that assumes that that child understands the subject at hand is the greatest mistake made by well-intended religious zealots when teaching young children. Such things as lust, adultery, and coveting thy neighbor's wife were unknown and incomprehensible to me. The lack of any concern regarding developmental or age appropriateness of the material being taught and the methodology being used resulted in a superficial knowledge of the subject by a disengaged learner. The many years I spent in Catholic school were years of mechanical repetition. Attending mass and going to confession were, as I said, things that I merely did. At times, however, there was some feeling behind these actions; fear of damnation, for example, was the underlying emotion for adhering to the doctrines of the Catholic Church. I was making sure to cover my bets. *If* there was a heaven, I wanted to make sure that I got there.

This skeptical acceptance of the Church's doctrines made things worse for me, because, as I often tell my students, I had my sister Angie, who could do no wrong, sharing the bed with me. Here she was, Mother Teresa herself, praying and paving her place in heaven, while I was a sure candidate for the fiery pit. No great sin had to be committed to become eligible for eternal damnation. The mere thought that there was not really a God or the slightest twinge of dislike for someone would be enough to make me feel that infamous Catholic guilt and assure me that Satan was waiting for me at the gates of hell. I resented the nuns for exposing me to such beliefs. Without their indoctrination, I would be but a poor ignorant soul, who would not be held accountable for not knowing the truth. As the nuns told us, he who does not know will not go to hell. Every time they slapped a child, pulled our hair, or administered a punishment in the name of not knowing the catechism, my fear of them increased, but so did my dislike for them and for what they represented.

How could people who were supposed to be so holy also be so mean? Although I resented the nuns and priests for inflicting me with these beliefs and the guilt and fear that came with them, I now realize and understand that they themselves were victims of what was taught to them. The intensity of their beliefs and faith manifested in life-altering commitments was not something that I ever experienced or wished to experience. Unlike Angie, I never desired to be a nun. The lifestyle, the discipline, and my lack of faith all contributed to this. Nonetheless, the overwhelming numbers of Irish nuns and priests in the church, as well as the celebration of Saint Patrick's Day and the overwhelming emphasis placed on Irish culture throughout my years in parochial school, made me wish that I were Irish. The lack of mention of a black saint or a Hispanic saint, and the emphasis placed on the salvation of souls in Latin America by European missionaries, contributed to the idea that heaven was reserved for those who were not Hispanic or black. The very image of God, or of Mary or Jesus, or any other blessed person was that of someone with blonde hair, blue eyes, and fair skin. I wished I were Irish to assure myself a place in heaven.

The irreverent and sacrilegious nature of my family worked to further enhance my disbelief in Catholicism. My uncle Miguel and my father had their own interpretations of the Bible, and they would constantly tell me things that shattered the beliefs taught in school. I remember not eating meat on Fridays because it was a mortal sin. My father, in an attempt to show me the absurdity of this belief, informed me that the only reason this was a sin was because Saint Peter, who was a fisherman, needed the business. So Jesus made it a sin to eat meat on Fridays. It all boiled down to economics. The Rubal interpretation of Christianity is unique. My uncle Miguel let me know that the reason Judas betrayed Jesus was because Maria Magdalena, who was his former girlfriend, had dumped him for Jesus Christ. Jealous and jilted, Judas was left with no alternative but to turn him in to the authorities.

As a child, the conflict between the culture of my home and the culture of the church became even more intense when John Kennedy, whom the priests and nun saw as a hero and the closest thing to a saint, was elected president. My father disliked Kennedy intensely. He constantly referred to Kennedy as the bootlegger's son. The Bay of Pigs invasion, which threatened my father's hero Fidel Castro, contributed to the intensity of this conflict. My spirituality was now being molded by politics, allegiances, and my confusion about what was the truth.

Chapter Three

Middle Education
Moving on Up

Alma

When I was in the fourth grade we moved out of the projects. My mother, who after many years of being at home had decided to start working again, arrived at a solution that would provide Angie and me with the supervision we needed while she was not home, and simultaneously relieve her of some of the household chores. Carmen Vega, an elderly woman who was in need of a place to live, came to live with us. In exchange and for a minimal amount of money, Carmen took care of us and tended to our home while my mother worked. Carmen's children had already grown up and moved away, and they did not want her living with them, so Carmen was very happy to live with us. Our home became a place where she was loved once again; she felt like a part of the family. Since our apartment was not large enough to provide her with a bedroom, my parents left the projects in pursuit of a bigger home and a better life.

I would later come to find that this move from Patterson Projects was the end of the happiest and most innocent years of my childhood. The abrupt turn that my life would take would transform me into an adult inside a child's body. My thoughts of play, fun, and friends I was forced to trade in for thoughts focusing on sickness, discomfort, and pain. Everything changed. What was once a rather stable and secure existence for our family was suddenly haunted by a myriad of problems.

Prior to the move, my mother, who always saw the glass as half full, told Angie and me that we were moving to this great apartment in a building that was similar to a private house, in a country-like setting and in a neighborhood that had a gorgeous park. For an instant, I had envisioned moving into the kind of neighborhood that I had seen in the TV show *Father Knows Best*. I imagined white picket fences and beautiful backyards and front lawns, at every house for as far as I could see. I felt like my most cherished wish was finally coming true.

The truth was that we were moving from one part of the South Bronx to another. The gorgeous park was Crotona Park, a deteriorated hole plagued by crime. Day or night, this was a dangerous park; name the crime and it was being committed in Crotona Park. From day one of moving into our new neighborhood, Angie and I were warned not to enter that park, especially since we were young girls who were new to the area. The building that we were moving into was an eight-family four-story structure that was falling apart, and the location of the building could not have been more of an inconvenience, for all of us. But I felt especially bad for my mother, whose body was riddled by three kinds of arthritis. Every day she had to climb a huge hill to get to the subway. I still cannot fathom how she managed.

My father, who worked in Long Island at the time, had no major highway at his disposal, and as for Angie and me, there was no Catholic school nearby, which meant that we had to take a bus to school. This distance from the school that we went to affected our lives in many ways. The daily commute was one thing, but what caused the most problems for Angie and me was that our school was in a community that was foreign to us. This made us outsiders. None of my classmates lived in our neighborhood, and our school was in a predominantly Italian neighborhood in the Belmont area of the Bronx, a neighborhood that had very few minorities. I never thought this would happen, but I found myself yearning for those days when we lived in the projects.

And things only got worse. Our new landlords, Santiago and Helen, were alcoholics and were actively negligent in their duties as homeowners. The condition of the building was horrendous. There were wood floors that were so old that our feet would sink when they made contact with the most trafficked areas, and most of the windows had been painted shut and were impossible to open. Since the alcohol kept our landlords feeling no pain, they assumed that everyone else was also feeling the same. In the middle of winter, we would have no heat for weeks. It was so cold that we couldn't look out the windows because every pane of glass had become sheeted with ice. Angie and I would sleep in our clothes and sit around the TV with our coats and hats on. It was so cold that we took it upon ourselves not to take off our pajamas for Sunday mass. We would simply roll up our pajamas, put on socks, and go to church.

One day, Mrs. Matos, a lady who also attended mass with her daughter, invited us to her house for breakfast, an event that we welcomed after fasting from the night before in order to receive communion. It was not until we got to Mrs. Matos's home that we remembered that we had our pajamas on under our coats. The lady kept trying to convince us to take off our coats, but we explained that we were still cold from outside. As we sat at the kitchen table with sweat dripping down our faces, we finally gave in and took off our coats. There we stood totally exposed, with a lot of explaining to do.

Except for the additional room to house the new member of our household, there was no reason for making this move. In retrospect, the change must have been a desperate attempt by my mother to save her marriage or to reinvent her life. The apartment was so cold that during the first winter, my mother fell ill twice with pneumonia. During the second winter, she found herself fighting the same sickness. The doctor told her that she needed to move to an apartment with heat, because her lungs could not tolerate another winter without heat. Carmen announced that she wanted to go to the Dominican Republic to visit her family, and we began apartment hunting.

One day my mother dressed us in our Sunday best and we went looking for a new place to live in the vicinity of the Grand Concourse, which at the time was a predominantly white neighborhood known for its wonderful apartments. As we sat in the real estate office, I could hear my parents talking to each other in Spanish about the kind of apartment that they wanted. Since Carmen was not going to be with us, they were willing to move into a two-bedroom. The agent who was sitting on the other side of the barrier did not even ask my parents to enter. He spoke to them from his desk. "What do you want?" he asked coldly. My father explained in his best broken

English that we were looking for a two-bedroom apartment. "We have no apartments for rent," said the agent, and that was that. That day we went to several real estate agents, with the same results. On the way home, my parents agreed that we should stay in the neighborhood where we lived because no one in a predominantly white neighborhood was going to rent to a Puerto Rican family.

So we stayed in our neighborhood and moved into a new apartment up the same hill that my mother climbed every morning on her way to the subway. It was an old building that was heated by coal and, unlike our former icebox, there was an excess of heat. In fact, we had to open the windows because the heating system seemed to be unregulated. The downfall of living in this building was our neighbors, the kind with four legs, dark gray fur, and long, thick tails. They were the kind of neighbors that invited themselves to any apartment with heat, and as I said, we had lots of heat. One could not spend any considerable time in the apartment without coming across one of them. The building was totally infested.

For a young person such as myself, who had never seen a roach or a mouse until moving into this building, this was quite a traumatic experience. At all times we would sit with our feet off the ground, for fear that one of our neighbors would suddenly show up unannounced. What a senseless move this was! We left the icebox only to move to a rat palace. When I finally got my own room, I was too scared to sleep in it because the mice and rats would keep me awake at night scratching and making noises as they ran through the bedroom. One night when my parents went out, Angie and I moved my bed into her room, and I was finally able to get some sleep. I had my big sister to protect me against the attack of the super rats.

School was just another source of anxiety. As one of four minorities in a predominantly white class of forty girls, I felt disengaged from school activities. The feeling of not belonging that would always be present throughout my life rose to prominence while attending St. Martin of Tours School. For three years, Lillian, Alba, Esmerelda, and I, the only nonwhite students, were seated in the back of the room. In retrospect, we did what we were told and required little attention. None of us played any major role in the class activities. As I sat in the back, I viewed year in and year out those who were the teacher's pets, those who were disliked by her, and, of course, us, those who were nonexistent. My seat represented the marginal neighborhood with Linda, the poor white trash of the class, seated right in front of me. Ironically, the four of us were situated according to our skin gradation. The person with the lightest skin, me, sat closer to the front, with Lillian following me and the one with the darkest skin in the very back of the room. I often wonder if Mrs. Terrilli or Ms. Canata consciously arranged our seats in this order or whether our being situated in a kind of ghetto was just a coincidence. Whatever the case was, our seating served to disengage us from the rest of the class. We were rarely called on and rarely volunteered for anything. Special events, such as school pageants and plays, came and went with us having very little interest or involvement. Although I would like to think that there was no malice intended in the way that we were treated, I know that teachers are not beyond making decisions based on certain attitudes and beliefs that they themselves may be unaware of. This may account for the fact that not one of the four of us during this time was ever selected to be a class monitor. We never executed a key role in a school play; we were never acknowledged for anything that we did well. Positive reinforcement, which is a tool used by teachers to mold the behavior of students, was nonexistent as far as the four of us were concerned. Our nondisruptive behavior was primarily one thing—the avoidance of pain. The fear we had that one of those nuns or lay teachers would bang our heads against the wall or slap our faces contributed to our nonexistence in the ghetto corner of the class.

Nevertheless, this forced seating bonded us in a way that we could not foresee. Twenty years later, Lillian would be the witness at my wedding, and we remained best friends until her premature death in her mid-thirties. Our friendship was the result of our hanging out after school. Her family was very much like mine. Both of her parents were hard-working people who were trying to provide for their children the best they could. Her mother owned a beauty parlor and her father was a merchant marine, who at times was gone from their home for months at a time. We did not speak much about what was going on in our lives, but when we did, the similarities were mind-blowing. Both of our fathers were psychologically and emotionally absent from our lives, while our mothers were trying to keep the environments at home intact in a culture and at a time when divorce was frowned upon. The difference in the two homes was that Lillian's was plagued by domestic violence, whereas emotional abuse in the form of silence and denial was what plagued mine.

It became clearer and clearer to me that my home was not the happy place that I thought it was. I am not sure why prior to this period I envisioned my home the way that I did. Perhaps it was the lack of obvious signs such as fighting or arguing. Maybe in my ignorance all the signs were there, but as a child I thought that this was normalcy. Or it could be that once my parents really did love each other and we really did have a happy home, but this phase of our lives had come to an abrupt end. A more likely reason would be that maybe my age allowed me to focus on the situations of others and therefore my awareness of what other persons were confronting was heightened. The circumstances of my life had forced me to focus on things that were not about me. In any event, my father's daily presence at home became shorter and shorter, while his absences during the weekends and at night became greater. Furthermore, with Carmen gone, Angie and I were virtually unsupervised, and it seemed that my mother was coming home later and later. Angie and I quickly became responsible for the upkeep of our home and for our performance in school. My mother, who could barely make it through a day at work, would come home and lie in bed while she saturated her body with liniment and covered her joints with a heating pad, only to have to wake up and go to work the next morning.

Angie

I would describe the period immediately following the move from the projects as the commencement of my ethnic wounding. It coincided with my entrance into the sixth grade. Feelings of shame about being Hispanic, poor, and different originated at this time. While living in the projects I did not feel different from anyone else. Although we were poor, we never *felt* poor, because everyone was in the same boat. The projects were the great equalizer.

The new school, St. Martin of Tours, was more modern and better equipped than my former school, St. Rita's, but its facilities could not help me cope with what I went through every day at that school. Having to spend grades six through eight commuting to a school that was in a predominately middle-class Irish and Italian neighborhood had a much more destructive impact on my self-esteem than did life in the projects.

I was the only Hispanic in my class. Thus, I became the "exception" or Puerto Rican who was unlike the rest of the typical Hispanics. One of the nuns who was especially fond of me suggested that I not refer to myself as Puerto Rican. It sounded better, more polite, to say that I was Spanish; especially since, as she told me, I "did not look or act like a Puerto Rican." No one could tell what I was, she reasoned, so why should I advertise it?

Prior to transferring to St. Martin's, I had never associated being Puerto Rican with anything negative. But the subtle message I got from that nun who considered herself looking out for me was that because I was smart, a high achiever, and had light skin I did not represent my ethnic group. I was not like the rest of the Puerto Ricans, and I would be doing myself a great disservice by publicly identifying myself with *them.*

I soon learned that the parents of my new girlfriends were also more receptive to their daughters bringing home a Spanish girl rather than a Puerto Rican. Puerto Ricans ruined neighborhoods; they were loud, dirty, colored, and dangerous. They usually carried knives and could not speak English. I remember going with a group of girlfriends to someone's home and not being allowed to enter with the rest of my schoolmates because the parents did not want Puerto Ricans in their home. I had to wait outside until they came out. I repressed this incident for many years. It came to light during an exercise at a Cultural Diversity training in which I took part decades later. I had shut down emotionally and went through similar childhood experiences like a sleepwalker. It was a way of not having to deal with the deep hurt and shame I felt. It never occurred to me to speak up or refuse to wait outside or even to discuss it with someone. Instead, I buried my feelings.

I can trace the origin of a lifelong sense of inferiority and unworthiness to this time. I compared myself to these new classmates and always seemed to fall short. They lived in private homes that had front and back yards. My dad, unlike their fathers, was an atheist. He was not a member of the Holy Name Society like the fathers of my classmates, and my mother never went to church. During that time, she worked out of our home. The other mothers were housewives who cooked roast beef and potatoes. My mother cooked rice and beans with fried plantains. My father did not speak English properly and was rarely at home; his views were politically incorrect. His hero was Fidel Castro. I was taught in school that Castro was a dictator, a traitor, and above all else, a Communist. At home Fidel was the great liberator who dared to fight American imperialism. Any discussion with dad about Fidel turned into a major argument. I remember coming home from school one day and repeating to my father some minute piece of information I had learned, and immediately he went into a tirade about Yankee propaganda, the evils of capitalism, the inadequate American educational system, and the corruption of the Church. Needless to say, my parents were not Ozzie and Harriet.

My only claim to fame was that I was a good student, and I received acknowledgment and recognition for this from teachers and fellow students. Academic achievement was what made me special, and because of this, doing well in school became very important to me, as a way to receive acceptance into this new environment. The excitement of learning was there, but it took a backseat to the need to prove myself and to belong. Unfortunately, the more I succeeded academically, the more I felt the pressure to continue to succeed. I became so identified with being a straight-A student that I felt it was the only thing I had to offer. Without my grades I was nobody. Fear once again entered my life, the fear of academic failure and not living up to being the Puerto Rican who was an exception.

As I got older, enduring the surprised reactions people had when they learned that I was Puerto Rican was taking its toll on me emotionally. I was oddly conflicted. On the one hand, I understood that the intention of some was actually meant to be positive; they felt that they were giving me a compliment, by saying something like, "Don't worry, you are not seen like the rest of your people; no one would know to look at you. You can pass." These people had no idea that such sentiments exposed their prejudices. They were so sure they knew who the Puerto Ricans were and what they represented that they were convinced that I would be delighted to know that I was not being associated with the rest of them. They liked me well enough to allow me to enter their inner circle. After all, I was special and this specialness of mine worked to mask who I actually was. In fact, I was liked not *for* who I was, but *in spite of* who I was. As a result, my ability to fit in made me feel guilty about denying my identity. The price for belonging was a great one.

I do not remember inviting anyone from school to my home subsequent to the move from the projects. For one thing, they did not live near me and would have had to commute by bus, and I did not want anyone from school to see how I lived. Our apartment was shabby, cold, and rat-infested.

One day, my father brought his blind, eighty-something mother to live with us, and he expected my mother to take care of her. Francisca Espinosa, better known as *Abuela* Panchita, never liked my mother, so this was not an arrangement made in heaven.

Panchita had been a fiercely independent woman who had been saddled at an early age with raising her younger siblings when her mother died. She had had to take care of her father's bakery business when my great-grandfather was in an accident resulting in two broken legs. Panchita had assumed adult responsibilities at a very early age and was accustomed to being in charge. When her father remarried, it was a major battle to relinquish the household duties to her father's new wife. Panchita's displacement by her stepmother triggered her to seek a career as a nurse. Francisca, already an experienced caregiver, became the first registered nurse of Puerto Rico. She was an unusual woman for her times. She chose a profession that for conservative Puerto Rico circa the late 1890s was very daring and scandalous. After all, she saw naked men!

Panchita traveled to New York City to work in the Skin and Cancer Hospital in 1901. She was brave, strong, and gutsy. When she returned to Puerto Rico several years later to tend to one of her sisters who was ill, Panchita was urged by numerous physicians to stay on the island because of her valuable and much needed nursing skills. In those days, Panchita not only sanitized and prepared operating rooms in country settings, she served as the anesthesiologist and assisted with the actual surgery. Panchita worked with the most respected physicians of Puerto Rico, and her clients included some of the island's most famous and wealthy inhabitants. Despite such accomplishments, in certain circles she was considered to have gone beyond the social norms by engaging in such a profession.

Also amazing for that time was the fact that she married in her late thirties, after many years of being a professional woman. A woman was an old maid if she was in her twenties and not yet married. She had her first child at the age of thirty-eight! Her husband, who was a very conservative Spaniard, insisted on her giving up nursing for a more appropriate profession. When they moved to the Dominican Republic, she opened up a small candy factory to help her husband, who ended up being not very successful in the lumber business he launched. Panchita had acquired pastry and candy making skills as a youngster and used these skills throughout her life. I remember her outstanding cakes, ladyfingers, flan, and dulce de leche. She was very artistic. Cakes were decorated with beautiful birds, angels, or flowers. For one birthday party with a Halloween theme and celebrated in late October (the month in which Alma and I were born), she created a masterpiece. It looked like a three-tiered wedding cake, but it was light orange in color and decorated with edible witches, goblins, and pumpkins.

She also had a vast knowledge of medicinal herbs and home remedies.

After her husband was involved in a mysterious and fatal car accident, she returned to Puerto Rico to raise her two adolescent boys, my father, Manolo, and my Uncle Miguel. She never remarried. Being a single mother in her day was also unusual and raised many eyebrows, especially in my mother's conservative family.

When I was a small child, *Abuela* Panchita lived on the Upper West Side of Manhattan. She had a large apartment with many bedrooms, which she rented to boarders. She was a very lean woman with an amazingly straight posture who moved with a quick and purposeful gait. You could tell that she had never been a beauty, but she had a remarkably attractive and youthful figure until her death at age 104. She remained flexible and nimble to the end. She also had dazzling hazel eyes, frizzy hair, and a brown complexion.

Her kitchen had a large round wooden table with a marble top that she used to roll out her dough and create those magical pastries. There were always delicious smells of cakes, orange or lemon peels, and drying herbs drying hanging from the ceilings. *Abuela* Panchita always seemed to be doing something. In fact, I cannot remember her ever being still. She still worked as a private duty nurse, baked for special clients, and tended her boarders well into her eighties. *Abuela* Panchita was multitalented, strong, independent, and brave.

She was also cold, unaffectionate, stubborn, and argumentative. When she lost her eyesight at the age of eighty-eight, she never got over it. For an independent woman who was used to making her own way in the world, blindness was very difficult. When she came to live with us, she was bitter and angry. A soft, cuddly grandmother type she was not. She could yell, scream, and curse with the best of them. She never hesitated to reprimand my father when she felt the need. It was quite amazing to see this little woman pointing her finger and yelling at my much taller father, and he never argued back. "*Por favor, mama!*" was his response.

Because my father spent less and less time at home, however, her wrath fell on my mother, who in Panchita's eyes was part of the arrogant Bryan family who treated her with disdain.

By then my mother was working full-time and it was very difficult for her to deal with *Abuela* Panchita, run a household, raise two kids, work full-time, and deal with her illnesses. When my mother got pneumonia, she had no support from my father. She relied on me, a thirteen-year-old, to cook and care for my grandmother while I desperately tried to take care of her. My resentment of my dad flared up and resulted in a very angry and violent confrontation, after which my mother decided to seek a new life in Puerto Rico without my father.

Chapter Four

Adolescence
Return Migration/Back to *la patria*

Alma

A dolescence is a time of searching for one's identity, a reformulation of how one views life; it is a period that is very often looked upon as a difficult but somewhat happy time. When I think back to my own adolescence, I am reminded of periods of great change and of sadness and torment. There were no "best of times" to balance out the "worst of times" that seemed only to worsen with each new day.

During the spring of my sixth grade of schooling, my father and mother separated. That summer, my mother took my sister and me to Puerto Rico to start a new life without my father knowing about it. This was very difficult for me, because I was the only one from my immediate family who was speaking to my father. My parents did not separate amicably.

As poor people, my parents did not have the long slew of professionals usually associated with marital separations of the wealthy. There were no family counselors, therapists, legal agreements, or any other means to ensure an easy transition. There was no distribution of wealth, merely the distribution of bills. My father took his clothes, records, and books and was quickly gone. There were, however, plenty of intense feelings of anger and a great deal of blame and resentment on all sides.

My feelings were of deep sadness for a life that was quickly disintegrating. I felt very much alone in a home that was plagued with heartbreaks and sorrow. I missed my father and fantasized that all this would come to an end. But all signs led me to believe that these fantasies would never be realized.

Before my mother moved us to Puerto Rico, the separation made me closer to my father. He now seemed to be more engaged in my life, and every weekend we would go somewhere and spend the day together, something that was rarely done prior to the separation. He would pick me up in front of our palace of rodents and take me to Coney Island, Freedom Land, the beach, and many other places.

My mother knew that he would object to our move to Puerto Rico, so she made me promise that I wouldn't say a word. This was a no-win situation for me. It was very difficult to say good-bye to him on that last day in New York. We spent the day at Jones Beach together. There was not much to say to each other, so he read me excerpts from the *New York Times* in his unintelligible broken English, as he always did when he did not know what to say.

It must have been something negative about Kennedy, whom he referred to as the "son of a bootlegger," or it was something good about Castro whom he admired because of his anticapitalist stance. Either way, it was of no interest to me. However, I paid attention and pretended to understand and care about what he talked about. I had done it before; it was my way of relating to him and being close to him.

For a man who did not know how to be a husband or a parent, this was as good as it got. The way that he interacted with us consisted of his talking about *his* interests, whether the topic was world politics, boxing, baseball, ancient history, Simon Bolivar, tango, art, or any other subject that was important to him. This was my father's way of reaching out to us. And we returned his love by being engaged.

I now know that he was a victim of a marriage that should never have happened, and he was a product of a culture and generation that did not cultivate the greatest husbands or fathers. It wasn't the perfect situation and he wasn't the ideal father, but he was the only one I had. He wasn't Robert Young on *Father Knows Best*, but he was better than many of my friends' fathers who were always at home, controlling everyone's life and sometimes even engaging in violence. I had the best of all worlds. I had a father whom I knew and at the same time one I did not have to deal with, because he was never at home long enough for us to truly interact. Who could ask for anything more? He was exciting, funny, eccentric, attractive, and unpredictable. When I was old enough to understand certain things, my mother would often say to me, "Your father makes a better lover and friend than he does a father or husband."

As I kissed him good-bye in the car, I could not help thinking that I might never see him again. As I left the car, I quickly entered the building and could feel the tears rolling down my face. It was such a betrayal, and I was the one doing the betraying. For sure I would be sent to hell for this, and there was no time for confession. We were leaving for Puerto Rico the next day.

At the airport there were many families also migrating back to the island. After all, this was a period in Puerto Rican history that was marked by the greatest numbers of natives who had settled on the mainland returning back home to their beloved Borinquen, the Indian name for Puerto Rico.

Many of these people were returning to their homeland as poor as they had left, after many years of working in sweatshops. For them, the American dream had not been realized. Instead of the split-level home with a car in every driveway that they had idealized when coming to the United States, their American dream had been transformed into an endless nightmare of long, cold winters, crime-ridden neighborhoods, deplorable housing conditions, and far too much attention focused on race.

Their return was an attempt to provide their children with a better life, which, ironically, was the reason they had left Puerto Rico. This was yet one more attempt to realize those unfulfilled expectations. As one of those children, I was both sad and excited. The first thing I was going to do was to write my father and let him know that I was okay.

Our flight to Puerto Rico was the last flight of the night on Pan American, a flight usually traveled by nontourists because of the low fares. We left New York at midnight and landed in Puerto Rico around four o'clock in the morning.

As we exited the plane, we could feel the intense humidity that instantly mutated my sister's curly hair into an Afro. Then, as if from nowhere, we were being attacked by mimes, which are these almost microscopic creatures that sting you on every part of your body. I was told that the mimes and mosquitoes knew who was not from the island and would attack these people with a greater intensity. Within minutes my legs were bleeding from scratching at the insect bites.

Surprisingly, there were no relatives to meet us at the airport. So the three of us got our bags, called a taxi, and went to my grandmother's house. As we drove through the streets of Santurce at daybreak, I could feel the pain from the insect bites burning my legs, and I could not help but wonder if this move was a good one. I certainly hoped that it was. I wanted everything to work out for us, because if it didn't work out, New York was very far and too expensive to go back to. Please God, let this not be one of my mother's sugarcoated dreams.

My grandmother greeted us at the door and showed us to our room. Her apartment was on the second floor of a house situated in one of the busiest areas of the city. As we entered the room and saw that the bed was covered by a mosquito net, I knew that this move to the island was indeed an adventure. What I was not sure of was how ready I was for such an event. A few hours later, I was woken by a newspaper boy yelling *Imparcial*, *El Mundo*, and the sound of vendors selling *leche* (milk), *huevos* (eggs), *platanos* (plantains), *aguacate* (avocados), *pan* (bread), and many other items. They would walk through the streets, many of them without shoes, yelling at the top of their voices so everyone could be alerted. I woke up in a bath of sweat, covered with mosquito bites all over my body. The pain of the bites was intolerable. Needless to say, my first experience in a mosquito net was not the best.

During the short time that we spent at my grandmother's, I got to know her quite well. She would crochet while she rocked in her rocker and spoke to us about what wonderful people our aunts, uncles, and cousins were. She also talked about everything from religion to the latest gossip. During one of those talks, she mentioned Doña Panchita, my paternal grandmother, whom she referred to as being *una persona de color*, a colored person.

I knew that my father's mother had brown skin, curly hair, and green eyes, but I did not know that she was a Negro. Where I came from, there were only Negroes, Americanos, and Spanish and/or Puerto Ricans, and I was classified in the latter category. Race was not a big deal for us. We knew that we looked different from each other, but it just was not given much importance. We were all Spanish or Puerto Rican and that was it. Now I had one more thing to contend with. I was now a Puerto Rican of color.

However, my grandmother let me know quickly that this was also incorrect. I was *de alla*, from "over there," and so I really wasn't Puerto Rican. After all, my Spanish was quite poor, and I knew nothing about Puerto Rico. At the time, I was one of thousands of children migrating from New York to Puerto Rico who were met with the same kind of greeting that both Angie and I got. We were not considered true Puerto Ricans.

To add to the problem, this was a time when Puerto Rico was moving from an agrarian society to an industrial one, resulting in the development of large cities. With every great social upheaval comes both good and bad, and guess who was blamed for the bad. As the crime statistics went up, the drug trafficking increased and juvenile delinquency was on the rise, and those from *alla* were blamed.

I had come so far to find out that I was a Negro person without a country, and now I was being blamed for the disintegration of Puerto Rican society. For an adolescent who was in the midst of finding her identity, this was overwhelming. Every day there was a new, life-altering factor to deal with.

Angie

The move to Puerto Rico precipitated the other component of my ethnic wounding—the rejection I felt from my own people, which included my own family. Ever since we had moved from the projects, I had longed for the feeling of fitting in, a feeling of community. My head was filled with dreams of a beautiful Caribbean island and a family that would welcome me with open arms. For years, my mother had lulled us to sleep with stories of the *flaboyan* trees, Luquillo beach with water so clear that you could see your toes and water so warm that you could swim for hours without getting cold. She described the mountains, the delicious fruits, the rainforest, and the endless sunshine. She came from a large family, and I had heard stories about aunts and cousins whom I longed to meet. They sounded like they were so united and loving.

What a shock to find out that we were considered a burden rather than beloved members of a family. *Abuela* (grandmother) Mercedes, my maternal grandmother, was very unkind. She was a short, plump woman with snow-white hair, brown eyes, and a very light complexion—so light that it was colorless. She was a little bow-legged and walked with a slight limp. I can still picture my first Christmas in Puerto Rico. Alma and I were the only grandchildren who did not receive Christmas presents from her that year. It is still difficult to fathom how she could feel right about being so cruel to her grandchildren.

She criticized us for everything. "They were raised in New York, so what could you expect?" she would moan to her cronies as she rocked in her rocking chair and crocheted her endless doilies. "They cannot even speak Spanish properly." I became so discouraged that I stopped trying to speak Spanish, because I was constantly being corrected. My pronunciation and verb agreement always seemed to be wrong. One thing she especially hated about us was the very deep tans we developed after visiting the beach. She could not understand why we would want to go out of our way to darken our skins. She insisted at one point that we walk with a parasol to keep the sun off our complexions.

The truth was that *Abuela* (grandmother) Mercedes Arana Roig was obsessed with class and race. She was a woman who had been born into some wealth—at least by Caribbean standards. Her parents' people came from the north of Spain (Asturianos and Basques). They were landowners who lived comfortably. Mercedes grew up with servants and a certain social status, and she married well. My maternal grandfather, Tomas Bryan Suffront, was a judge for the District of Aguadilla. He had been educated in Spain as an attorney. *Juez* (Judge) Bryan had inherited a 500-acre coffee plantation that was worked by sharecroppers. These sharecroppers were actually freed slaves, many of whom had taken the last name Bryan as a symbol of respect for the family that granted them their freedom. Tomas's mother, my great-grandmother, had been from a French Royalist family who had settled in Martinique but were forced to flee to Puerto Rico when Napoleon came back to power. Dona Suffront spoke Spanish with a French accent, according to my mother's account. My great-grandfather was born in Puerto Rico, but his roots were in England.

Abuela Mercedes lost her husband when he drowned rescuing one of their nine children. Her oldest child, Tomas junior, about twenty years of age at the time, took over the running of the plantation. His lack of experience in managing a large plantation, coupled with a devastating hurricane that hit the island and the severe economic depression of the time, resulted in the loss of the property. She spent the rest of her life lamenting the loss of her social standing and aspiring to return to its midst.

Mercedes had an incredible knowledge of the genealogy of the "good" families of the island. She could trace anybody's family history. For example, the Mendes family from the town of Lares was related to the Gonzalez family of Mayaguez by the marriage of their second cousin to the daughter of our second cousin. So-and-so came from a good family, *una familia buena*. Apparently, there were a limited number of "good" families on the island. Most of these families had land and wealth and were white.

I learned very quickly that my father's family was not in this "good family" category. Besides working in a bakery, *Abuela* Panchita was not a lady because of her scandalous profession. Nursing was akin to being a servant or whore.

Abuela Mercedes talked often about the necessary separation of the races. The inferior Negro should not mix with the superior whites. A drop of Negro blood would manifest sooner or later in one's family. Mercedes was a self-appointed expert on "fine" features, eye and skin coloring as well as hair texture. People had good hair (*pelo bueno*), bad hair (*pelo malo*), and suspicious hair (*pelo sospechoso*). Because my very curly and frizzy hair was in the category of suspicious, I was a vulnerable target. My hair was attributed to my father's side of the family. Alma and I were colored. According to Mercedes, Panchita had Negro blood; it was obvious not only from her hair but also from a close observation of her features. And this, of course, was bad. Most of her other grandchildren were blonde with light eyes. The few with dark eyes had straight hair and fine features.

She was particularly cruel to Yolanda, the wife of my cousin Rolando. *Abuela* Mercedes was furious that Rolando had married a mulatta. It did not matter that Yolanda was pretty, intelligent, and hard-working. I never understood what Yolanda saw in Rolando, who was very handsome with large green eyes but was always unemployed and a proverbial liar. He was lucky to get someone like Yolanda. My grandmother repeatedly snubbed Yolanda and made it clear that Yolanda was not welcome in her home. I was deeply ashamed of this behavior.

Alma

My grandmother's attitude and lack of generosity motivated us to look for an apartment. That sweet old lady who my mother always spoke so lovingly to me about turned out to be a witch, a bitch, a racist, and an elitist all rolled into one.

During the months of searching for an apartment, we lived for a brief period with my aunt Cheche. Cheche was a rather eccentric but good-hearted woman who managed to bring up four children, two of whom she supported through medical school. We finally found an apartment in a countryside rental development that was inaccessible to school, shopping, or anything but cows and pastures. It was a small apartment, but it had been newly constructed, and its location was one that was high and cool.

However, the apartment had no refrigerator or stove and we had no money to buy such luxuries. So for the first couple of months we found ourselves without such items. In a hot climate, not having a refrigerator made life very difficult. Eating became an adventure and a real challenge. Nevertheless, it was our home and we were happy and thankful for this.

The problem was that the only Catholic school that we could afford and that had space was in Trujillo Alto, a small town on top of a mountain, and because of the poor roads and transportation, our commute to and from school took several hours.

Catholic school was important because English was the language of instruction and the same books that were used in the States were also used on the island. This ensured us a quality education and assured us that if we returned to New York, we would not be held back, the way many Puerto Rican children were at the time.

Every morning Angie and I would wake up and take a *carro publico*, public car, at about 5:30 a.m. After a long ride, we would get off in Rio Piedras, where we would take another *carro publico* to Trujillo Alto. The ride to Trujillo Alto was an adventure. We would get into a car with a minimum of seven people in it, and along the road people would get out and be picked up. Since students paid less money, the drivers would accommodate more people in the back, so we were seated on top of one another. The car would then start up this winding road with steep falls. The men smelled of cologne, the countryside of cow manure, and the cars stank of gasoline.

By the time we got to the school, which was located at the top of this huge mountain, we were ready for CPR. To add to our daily torment, the nuns would make us attend mass every morning before class. This was the worst. I was willing to go to mass on Sunday, because failure to do so would put me in a state of mortal sin and ready for eternal damnation, but what was the sense of every morning? I was definitely not trying to win the prize for Catholic of the Year.

To add insult to injury, mass was conducted in Spanish by a gringo priest whose language was unintelligible. The religious service was impossible to follow for someone like me who was never taught to pray in Spanish, so all I could do was sweat while I thought of the trip that I had just endured and the return trip that was awaiting us.

On the first day of school, I was placed in a classroom on the first floor. The teacher was a young woman who could not control the class. No one paid attention to her and cross-conversations took place throughout the day. The unruliness, however, turned to chaos when a huge cow entered the classroom. Everyone started screaming, including me. This was just too overwhelming.

First, we were being thrown out of my grandmother's house because there was no room for us, and every day we were expected to embark on a journey in order to attend school, only to be confronted with a priest giving a mass that could not be understood. Now I was being asked to contend with farm animals in my classroom. Something very wrong was occurring in my life. Please God, take me back home to El Bronx. I'll take my chances with the roaches, rats, muggers, child molesters, broken-down apartments, and cold winters. I was longing for a school that was not on another planet, a home of our own, a language that I could speak, and a community that was accepting of who I was. Soon after our relocation to our new rural apartment, my cousin Milva moved into a building on the next street with her three children as well as my grandmother. After asking us to leave her home, my grandmother had decided that her apartment was not large enough to house my cousin Milva and her children, who had come to Puerto Rico while her husband, a sergeant in the Marine Corps, was doing a tour in Okinawa. So my grandmother closed her apartment and came to live with Milva in the same housing development that we lived in. Furthermore, my Uncle Carlos moved across the street with his wife and three children while they awaited the construction of their new custom-built home.

The thought of living near our relatives was inviting to us. As kids who had never lived with family, we welcomed the opportunity to have them become part of our lives. In New York we had distant cousins, but we had never had the opportunity to get to know our "real relatives." However, we soon realized that our desire to be part of this family was overshadowed by all kinds of issues related to race and class.

Little did we know that we were considered lower-class ghetto kids who were not worthy of playing with my Uncle Carlos's children, a determination made by his wife. She discouraged any interaction with us and would go out of her way to let us know that she was superior to all of us. There were countless times that she would pass us by in her station wagon while we waited for a public car to take us into town.

She never came to see how we were or if we needed anything, a likely inquiry of a sick woman and two children who lived in the middle of a mountainside without any means of transportation. Birthdays and holidays were celebrated in their home, family reunions took place, but none of us were included. We could witness the number of cars arriving at their home and the laughter coming from within, and could only wish that we had been included.

Most importantly, food was thrown out when we had none to eat. Nevertheless, our sense of pride did not permit us to ask for anything. My mother, who had expected to be able to land a job easily in Puerto Rico because of her secretarial and bilingual skills, became so sick that she could not walk, and we had spent all the money that we had brought with us from New York.

During this same time, my father lost his job, because the airplane industry in which he worked had left New York for California. He also underwent surgery that required several months of recuperation, further contributing to our monetary problems. So Angie and I found ourselves in a desperate situation without money in the middle of this rural area.

To earn money, we would baby-sit as often and as long as we could. On occasion, we had to choose between eating or spending our money on transportation to get to school. I remember staying home from school because we did not have enough to get there. But our reputation as baby-sitters grew and our business boomed. At times we had more business than we could handle. At fifty cents an hour, a night's work could net six dollars between the two of us. On a good weekend we would work Friday, Saturday, and Sunday and make enough money to get through the week, not bad for a twelve-year-old and a fourteen-year-old.

Of all our surrounding relatives, Milva was the nicest. This was probably because this former debutante, who had attended the best schools in Puerto Rico and was given the best as a child, had fallen in love with a handsome Marine who was from the hills of Kentucky, and in doing so she went from a life of privilege to one of poverty.

Her life was not that of a rich person, but that of the wife of a Marine sergeant. She spent her life moving from North Carolina to South Carolina. To add to the problem, her husband was a heavy drinker who would frequently be demoted in rank. This resulted in his being a career soldier who could not go higher than a master sergeant. Her bad luck did not end there. She lost her first two children in tragic accidents. These occurrences, however, made her empathetic to what we were going through.

Whenever we were in her home, she was generous to us and always offered us something to eat. Milva would also invite me to the navy base, where we would spend time in the pool and I would help her take care of the kids. The base was a refuge for me. I would forget about the reality of my life and be greatly thankful for the dinner that Milva would buy me.

One late night after having spent a day at the navy base, I sat on our small balcony overlooking acres of farmland, gazing at the sky full of stars, and contemplated my experiences in Puerto Rico. A feeling of tremendous sadness overwhelmed me when I compared my life on the mainland to the one that I was having on the island. How sad it was that my mother's great feelings for her family were not reciprocated. What a disappointment. My mother always had a way of seeing only the good. In the same way that she told us what a great place we were moving to when we left the projects, and the place was a dump, she talked to us about what a great family she had and what a great place Puerto Rico was.

I also missed my father dearly. My mother and Angie had a very special relationship, of which I was not a part. I was not intentionally excluded, but that was my experience. The intense feelings that my mother and Angie had against my father were not mine, and maybe this is what led to my isolation. Whatever the reason, I felt that I was not part of their very special bond. So I found myself alone in a place that I did not feel a part of.

I was not welcomed in Puerto Rico, and in New York being a Puerto Rican was no picnic. In New York, Puerto Ricans were referred to as spics, and it was no secret that we were considered inferior to many of the "*Americanos*." I was not an "*Americana*" and I was not a Negro. Who was I?

It became apparent to me that I was a Puerto Rican from New York, a species different from those who came from the island. We saw life differently. In the Bronx we were all poor. No one cared about what you did for a living, what your last name was, or what your ancestry was. In Puerto Rico, you couldn't be introduced to someone without an interrogation. What is your last name? What town are you from? Such an inquiry would define who you were and would place you in your appropriate social standing. In Puerto Rico, I met in my family alone attorneys, teachers, engineers, and artists.

I can't remember when I first heard the term *Nuyorican* to refer to persons like myself, but the essence of what this term represents is what I felt. This was not my homeland. I was from *alla*. And that was where I wanted to be, the land of White Castle hamburgers, candy stores, Yankee Stadium, subways, Alexander's department stores, the Bronx Theatre, the Hunts Point Palace, the Polo Grounds, and good pizza, not the crap that they sold here.

School in Puerto Rico

Angie

Despite the difficulty of beginning high school in a new environment, and having to commute long distances and interact in Spanish, my high school experience in Puerto Rico was positive.

El Colegio de la Santa Cruz was located in a semirural community about a twenty-minute ride from Rio Piedras. It consisted of a grammar school and a high school. The high school had about seventy students total. Four Franciscan nuns served as the faculty. The only Puerto Rican nun, Sister Ramon, was the homeroom teacher for the freshmen. The rest of the nuns came from the Midwest. Sister Ramon was my Spanish, literature, and physical education teacher. The rest of the curriculum included algebra, English, science, social studies, and religion.

It was painful at first, because I was called *la gringa* or *la Americana*. Before long, however, I realized that the term was used to distinguish me as the new kid. The natural thoughtfulness and kindness of my fellow students took over. Students did not have a need to correct my Spanish, so my self-consciousness disappeared and the ability to communicate soon improved. By the end of the school year, I was elected class president.

Conversational Spanish was one thing, but doing academic work on the high school level without a background in written Spanish was another. Luckily, most of my classes were taught in English using American textbooks. Spanish, religion, and literature were conducted in Spanish. Although I was tutored on occasion, generally the expectation was that I would get it eventually. It was humbling for a straight-A student like myself to suddenly lag behind in any subject. On the other hand, I was not under the pressure I felt in New York to use my performance in school as a way of blending in. I was accepted with my limited Spanish skills. I felt free to be me—being me was acceptable.

There were many "firsts" in that school year. It was the first time I had a teacher who was Puerto Rican. It was the first time I went to school with all Puerto Rican students. Most astonishing was the fact that it was the first time I attended an educational institution without being in a constant state of fear—fear at first of the nuns, fear of being hated by my fellow students, and later, fear of not measuring up and being accepted. Formerly, Fridays were the best day of the week because I could look forward to two days without school and Sunday evenings were anxious times for me because I knew what was awaiting me the next day. School in Puerto Rico ended this pattern.

I remembered that learning could actually be fun, and I finally re-laxed. I remember much laughter and smiling that year. I felt accept-ed despite the fact that I did not have a great command of Spanish. I was delighted that Sister Ramon told jokes and that she did not mind students calling out their own jokes. Even the American nuns were relaxed and caring. There was not the feeling of competition that I was used to. My classmates took great delight in seeing my progress in Spanish. Without being told, students naturally helped each other. The class functioned like a team. We were engaged in cooperative learning before the term was coined. Individual class as-signments became class projects; I recall students sharing clippings and information with one another. I was doing a science term paper concerning the radio and was given information from several of my fellow students. Everyone wanted everyone else to succeed. It was as normal for me to help someone with English as it was for someone to help me with my Spanish. We were not in competition with each other; we were partners in learning. It did not feel good to do well if a classmate had done poorly. Interestingly, I do not recall even one student being humiliated or corporally punished in front of his or her peers. This was a common occurrence in New York.

Alma

Just as I was getting the hang of appreciating the combined smell of cow manure, cologne, and sweat on my daily escapade to Santa Cruz—and actually becoming more proficient in following the gringo-priest's mass—my cousin found an opening in a school in San Antonio. The new school was only half the distance of my cur-rent school. There was no room for Angie, so every morning we parted ways when we arrived at Rio Piedras and she continued on her journey.

San Antonio was considered one of the better schools. It housed a large middle-class population. We were taught by Franciscans, the same order of nuns found in Santa Cruz. Perhaps it was the noncompetitive nature and group orientation of the Puerto Rican culture that influenced the nuns' approach to education. I am not sure. But these nuns who came from the Midwest were much more informal and less authoritarian than those I had encountered in New York. The atmosphere of the school was warm and collegial.

All classes were conducted in English, except History of Puerto Rico and Spanish.

My experience was a good one. Volleyball and basketball were important activities, and surprisingly, every grade from seventh up had a female and a male team. I was a member of the volleyball and basketball teams and loved participating in these sports. We competed with other schools, an experience that I had never had but enjoyed greatly. Although my poor skills in Spanish marked the fact that I was not from Puerto Rico, there were enough of such students in my class to make me feel comfortable. They, too, were part of the return migration of Puerto Ricans from the States. Some were also separated from their fathers in the States, and all of us were trying to adjust to our new environment. We were not singled out because of where we were born.

At times, in fact, our classmates viewed us in a rather favorable manner as more savvy or worldly because of our origins. This reverence for us could possibly be seen as a by-product of the island's colonization and the internalization of values about what they were led to believe was superior. Nonetheless, our oneness as a class of students and my success in sports made me feel a part of this school in ways that I had never experienced at St. Martin of Tours back in the States. This sense of belonging was a blessing, since everything else in my life seemed to be in chaos.

One night while baby-sitting, I heard someone calling my name and Angie's name. It was a rainy and dark night, so I put the light on the rear balcony to see who was calling me. There was our downstairs neighbor telling me that my father was in her house. He was looking for us. At the time, Angie was baby-sitting somewhere else. Luckily, the people for whom I was working arrived at that instant and my work came to an end. I remember running through the grass and in the pouring rain to get to where he was. There he stood and there I was totally soaked and crying uncontrollably. We went into our apartment, where my father looked at our humble home. He quickly asked me where Angie was, and I told him that she was baby-sitting on the other street. Until what time would she be there? he asked. I shrugged my shoulders, maybe until two or three in the morning.

His face showed surprise and disapproval of our lifestyle. How does she get home? She walks home. By herself? Yes. But don't worry, I will go to her. That's what we usually do. Whoever finishes first joins the other so we don't have to walk alone. Then he said, It's very spooky in the country at night. Where is your mother? She's in the hospital. Why? What happened? I told him that Ricardo, my cousin the doctor, came to examine her and put her in the hospital. She stopped walking several weeks ago and she was in a lot of pain. So Ricardo came and institutionalized her.

The next day my father and mother talked in the hospital. I know that after his visit, he asked us if we wanted to go back to New York. We both said yes, but not without our mother. Several months later my mother, Angie, and I boarded a plane bound back to New York to once again be reunited as a family. Our year in Puerto Rico felt like a century. I was not returning back to New York as the same person I was when I had lived there before. Now at thirteen years old, I was an old lady in a young body. I had witnessed in that year the dark side of people.

Selfishness, poverty, sickness, racism, class discrimination, and much more were embedded in my memories. But all was not negative. I would miss Milva and the freedom that I had while in Puerto Rico. The sounds of the *coqui* at night and the skies full of stars would also be missed.

Chapter Five

Late Adolescence
Good-bye Isla del Encanto/Back to the Bronx

Eighth Grade

Alma

Our new home was on the top floor of a five-floor tenement near Westchester Avenue in El Bronx. The neighborhood consisted of a mixture of aging buildings and private houses. It was a neighborhood in transition, with the majority of white families fleeing due to the influx of blacks and Hispanics who were moving into the neighborhood. The apartment was a small one-bedroom with very little furniture. These cramped quarters became even more crowded when my paternal grandmother, who was now blind and senile, moved in with us. This forced Angie and me to share our room with her while my parents slept in the living room.

Just when we thought that we could not fit another person in the apartment, my alcoholic cousin Roland from Puerto Rico joined us. He had relocated from Puerto Rico and needed a place to live. He was given a piece of the floor near the entrance to call his own and a period of several months to get a job, save money, and move out. The overcrowded conditions were a concern but not an issue. We were grateful for what we had and now more than ever we knew from experience that things could be worse.

Angie entered the tenth grade at James Monroe High School. I started the eighth grade in a parochial school that was a short bus ride away. Before I entered Blessed Sacrament, the principal told me that I would have to be placed in seventh grade because the education I had received in Puerto Rico was inferior. She was particularly concerned about mathematics, because I would not be able to keep up with the rest of the class. My mother was about to concede to her suggestion when I interjected and explained to the principal that this was not correct.

I informed her that the same books that were used in Catholic schools in New York were used in Puerto Rico. Furthermore, I let her know that I would prefer to go to public school and be in the correct grade than be in Catholic school and in a lower grade. I could see this nun's piercing eyes as she sat there and pretended that there was no room in the eighth grade. She tried to convince me to sit in the seventh grade for a few weeks until maybe someone would move and there would be room. This sounded like a con, so I objected. I told my mother, "Come on, mom, let's go." At that moment, the principal gave up and let me go into eighth grade.

Ironically, at graduation I was the one who got the math award, the very subject that was used as an excuse for keeping me in seventh grade. Deep down I knew that this was about how this nun saw Puerto Ricans and not about the quality of education that I had received on the island. These assumptions and conclusions about the schools in Puerto Rico were made without any evaluation of what I knew or what I was taught. However, this was the kind of prejudice that I understood, and I knew how to handle it, unlike the racism and class discrimination I had encountered on the island.

While everyone in my class was preparing to go to Catholic high school, I knew that this was not to be in my future. We could barely afford this school, and Catholic high school was too expensive. The only reason that we were making this sacrifice was my mother's insistence that I graduate from Catholic school.

My eighth-grade nun, Sister Emeline, was furious at the fact that I was going to a public high school, and she kept me after school almost every afternoon and ridiculed me in front of class whenever she remembered that I was going to a public high school. She would ask me to stand in front of the class and would announce that I was going to St. James Academy, the home of the dummies, also known as James Monroe High School. She would then tell the class to take a good look at me because I was not going to amount to anything. I endured this humiliation on many occasions during that year. As graduation got closer and closer, it became easier and easier for me to deal with Sister Emeline's abuse, because my thoughts went progressively from embarrassment to the sheer joy of knowing that soon I would never again have to interact with a mean, bitchy nun.

I had had my fill of these women, and quite frankly I was looking forward to public school. I know that Sister Emeline was trying to break me down, but what she did not know was that I was as hard as nails. My experience in Puerto Rico provided me with the resources to deal with Sister Emeline without breaking down and thus letting her emerge the winner. The year I had spent in Puerto Rico had provided me with the ability to recognize what was important and what was not. As far as I was concerned, Sister Emeline was of very little significance.

Although I was very happy to be back in New York, the fact that my parents were reunited because of our insistence rather than their desire to be with each other was a reality that could not be ignored. Also, poverty, although not as extreme as it was in Puerto Rico, was still very much a part of our lives.

After the airplane industry left Long Island, my father found employment doing the only other thing that he knew how to do, drive a cab. He worked for a percentage of what the meter registered and the tips that he received. He drove for long hours and made only a fraction of what he had made as a tool and die machinist, without any benefits. Furthermore, my mother, who always tried to contribute financially to the household, was too sick to work. So Angie and I found ourselves attending high school in clothes discarded by people we knew and looking somewhat different from many of our classmates. I remember wearing skirts that were too tight or too long and classmates staring at me. I chose to ignore the stares and continued to excel in school despite the loneliness that I encountered in a high school where most of the students knew one another from junior high school or from their neighborhood.

High School

Angie

From ninth grade to tenth grade I underwent a major period of transition. I went from a small, semirural, parochial school to a large, urban public high school, James Monroe High School in the South Bronx. I was not placed in honor classes despite my excellent academic record. It was only when I completed my first semester at Monroe with a 95 percent grade point average and then insisted that I was allowed to join the Honor School. The Honor School at Monroe was composed of approximately 250 students, or the top 10 percent of the school's population. There were few minorities in the Honor School, which was mostly Jewish students and teachers; the student population of the entire institution was predominantly black and Hispanic.

Students in the Honor School were achievement oriented and focused on going to college. The cooperative spirit of Puerto Rico was replaced by fierce competition and single-mindedness. A few extra points earned by a classmate could change the test curve and negatively affect your final grade. Your performance could adversely affect someone else's success. Learning was no longer a win-win phenomenon, but by definition a win-lose experience; someone had to be on the bottom and someone had to be on top. I worked hard to be on top and graduated salutatorian.

I had always aspired to go to college, but I had no practical information of what it would take to get there. It was a vague goal. I did not know how much money it would require and the kind of grades it would take. My parents were not college graduates, so I had no mentors to pave the way. I began to investigate and soon realized that most students in the Honor School were going to one of the colleges of The City University of New York, which was free in those days. College was suddenly very doable and I looked forward to continuing my education at City College. A visit with my high school guidance counselor changed my focus. He claimed that with my grades and class standing I could go to any college in the country. It was the mid-sixties, colleges were looking to integrate their campuses with talented minorities, and I was a perfect candidate. He was very happy about the prospect of one of Monroe's students going to Harvard. Counselors who worked for Aspira of New York, the premier Puerto Rican educational and advocacy program at the time, were also delighted to have a young Puerto Rican girl with my educational background. I would be an excellent choice to open the path for other Puerto Ricans to break into Ivy League colleges. My father, who had never taken much interest in my education, was unexpectedly very excited about my going to Columbia University.

He bragged to his friends that I was accepted at Columbia before I even applied. Once again, I felt an inordinate amount of pressure to excel for others—my father, guidance counselor, teachers, and my fellow Puerto Ricans. What would happen if I did not get into these schools? I felt that I would disappoint everyone.

I worked very hard and got a solid education. The teachers in the Honor School were the best teachers I have ever had, bar none. They were knowledgeable, well prepared, and organized. They enjoyed teaching. They introduced me to new worlds. They challenged me and made me think. I recall being encouraged to select topics that were important to me for compositions. I delved into spiritual issues that have always interested me, such as the nature and purpose of suffering. I took advanced chemistry classes, honors physics, honors English, a special course in meteorology, world literature, and calculus. I made the honors dance program, but had to forgo it because it conflicted with honors chemistry. I was president of the Physical Science Research Club and a member of Arista (the honor society). I tutored other students and did research during lunchtime using a spectrophotometer. I was a candy striper for the American Red Cross and volunteered at the Lighthouse for the Blind.

Along with the intellectual excitement, I felt very pressured to get good grades because I was now on the fast track to the Ivy Leagues. On the outside, I looked very focused and clear, but in reality I was very unsure of myself and once again frightened to death that I would not make the cut and disappoint everyone.

Socially, I felt like an isolate. During high school I was not invited to parties or on dates. Many of the students had been in junior high school together, so there was an established social scene. I was the outsider. And once again, I became the exception—the only Puerto Rican. I was never invited out or to anyone's home, with the exception of a small group of friends who were also minorities. My best friends were a Cuban, an Ecuadorian, and a black. There were also two Jewish girls who transferred out of Monroe at the end of the tenth grade whom I kept in touch with for several years. We supported one another throughout the three years of high school. We were also the officers of the Physical Science Research Club. These friends represented a sanctuary for me. We studied together, did research together, argued about the meaning of life, shared books, listened to the Beatles, and went to the movies.

I did not feel judged by these friends and welcomed them to my home. Upon our return to New York, we moved to the one-bedroom apartment occupied by my father in the Sound View section of the Bronx, not far from James Monroe High School. During the fourteen-month separation, my father had had surgery and was out of work for some time. The airplane industry had relocated to the West Coast and my father was now driving a cab. We were starting all over again with few possessions, old furniture, and a limited budget. My mother's arthritis had flared up and she was unable to work, and because of our lack of finances, Alma and I wore my mother's old clothes to school. We also relied on hand-me-downs from a distant cousin who was working as a receptionist, as well as on my sewing skills, to get us through.

Abuela Panchita had returned to live with us, and she made my life very difficult. Besides being blind, she was senile. You never knew what to expect from her. I remember walking home with a boy from school. I was hoping to make a good impression on him. When we approached my apartment building, I noticed that there was a crowd gathered in front of the stoop. People appeared concerned about something or someone. When I came closer, I saw my grandmother, barefoot, dressed in only a cotton slip, holding an empty cup in her hand and begging for milk. Somehow she had managed to get down five stories despite her blindness. I dispersed the crowd by motioning with my hands that she was crazy. I tried to persuade her to return to the apartment with me, but she only screamed for the police. She claimed that she was being tortured. "*Llamen la policia. Me estan matando*" (Call the police. They are killing me). I had to stay with her for several hours until my father got home. He had to carry her up five stories with her screaming, kicking, and scratching him.

Need I say that I was completely embarrassed? My classmate, the boy I was walking home with, left before my father arrived.

On another occasion, a different schoolmate came over. He needed to borrow a book. Suddenly, my grandmother appeared out of the bedroom. She had the habit of roaming around the house and talking to herself. Sometimes it seemed that she was engaged in a conversation with someone else. These conversations were at times very calm but other times they could be very spirited and loud. She often cursed and told off the other person. "You son of a...," etc. After one such encounter, I asked her with whom she was speaking, and she told me that she was speaking to God.

She had the habit of plucking hair out of the right side of her head while she spoke to herself. She eventually became bald on this side. As she extended her left hand in front of her to help steer herself slowly across the apartment, depending on her mood, she might throw things that she would encounter in her walks. It was not unusual to find a broken planter or ashtray that she had come in contact with and had flung across a room.

Remarkably, when she came out of the bedroom on this occasion, she was very pleasant and calm; there were no loud voices and no throwing of objects. I was so relieved. I introduced her to my friend. As I conversed with him, I noticed that she had begun to pace in front of the front door. When it was time for my classmate to leave, I asked my grandmother to please move away from the door. She screamed that she would not because she was not stupid. She knew what we were up to, she told me. She knew that we were planning to elope. She would not allow it; I was too young. Then she flung herself across the front door and refused to let us out of the apartment. No amount of pleading or explaining or arguing or even threatening did any good. *Abuela* Panchita was in her late nineties, but she was spry and did not hesitate to kick, swing her fists, and scream her lungs out. My guest had to stay an extra two hours. Finally, my father arrived and was able to liberate my trapped and befuddled schoolmate.

It was very important to me that I had the type of friends who were able to accept my odd family and intrusive living arrangements.

Alma

At the end of my freshman year at James Monroe High School, where I was once again in the same school with Angie, who was now in eleventh grade, I received a full scholarship to the Calhoun School, a prep school on the Upper West Side of Manhattan. The scholarship was given to me for my outstanding performance in ninth grade. I had achieved the highest grade point average in my class. However, the underlying reason for this school's generosity was to diversify the school at a time when issues of race and equity were at the forefront of the national agenda.

Several weeks before beginning the tenth grade at the Calhoun School, I received an invitation to lunch at the home of my designated big sister, who lived on Fifth Avenue not far from the Metropolitan Museum of Art. The lunch was to take place on a Wednesday afternoon. When I showed my father, the cab driver in him was sparked. He said, "I know where that building is. That's the same building where Jacqueline Kennedy lives. Don't worry, I will take you because it's a Wednesday and that's my day off." I said to him, "That's okay. You don't have to bother. I'll go by subway." But he insisted. I thought I was going to die. How could I go to see someone who lived in Jacqueline Kennedy's building with a father who drove a run-down Rambler, and what was I going to do if he insisted on going in and talking in his broken English, which only I understood? It was bad enough that I had no nice clothes to wear and that I was going to be a nervous wreck, but now I had my father to contend with.

When the day arrived, I wore the nicest dress that I owned. I washed it and ironed it and made sure that every hair was in place. As we pulled in front of the building, the doorman approached our blue Rambler. He tried to open my door, but the car had been in an accident and it would not open. So my father got out of the car while I climbed over his seat and exited the car. I was very embarrassed and said goodbye to my father in English, a language that I never used when speaking to him. My father's accent was, undoubtedly, a marker of his ethnicity that in turn represented poverty, something that I did not wish to be associated with at that moment. Standing there on Fifth Avenue, I was overcome with shame, and my father's broken English was contributing to this feeling. The only other feeling that could overshadow the shame I felt was my guilt at feeling this way, guilt for not wanting to be who I was, and guilt on top of guilt when my father looked at me with that startled look when I spoke to him in English.

As I entered the lobby of the luxury building, I was questioned, announced, and directed to the correct elevator where a Hispanic male, who was clothed in a uniform, stood waiting to escort me to the correct floor. Surprisingly, when the elevator arrived there was a square hallway with only three doors. I stood there not knowing what door to ring.

The elevator operator pointed to the correct entrance, and I rang the bell. A black male dressed in a white uniform answered the door. He escorted me to this huge living room, where I sat for a few minutes admiring the baby grand piano, the paintings, the furniture, and the flowers that adorned this magnificent room. Although I had seen such rooms in the movies, I had never been in one. I was in awe of its beauty and elegance. The size of the room was also of a grand scale. In this room I could probably fit my family and still have room for my grandmother and Rolando. When my big sister Barbara entered, I was rather resentful because I was enjoying this experience and I was not finished surveying the entire contents of the room.

Nevertheless, we went to her room, where we talked and listened to music. It was also an impressive room with beautiful furniture and all items matching. While we talked, I fantasized that the room we were in was actually mine. Soon, her mother, Mrs. Lowenstein, entered and announced that lunch was ready. I was escorted to a huge dining room where I sat at the end of the table with her mother at the head and Barbara across from me. A short black woman served us broiled hamburgers from silver trays.

As I pretended to eat, a feat that was impossible because of my nervousness, Barbara's mother interrogated me about the name Rubal.

"I can't place that name," she said. "What kind of business is your father in?"

At that moment I died. This was not a question that I wanted to answer, so I chewed very slowly in order to buy some time and perhaps arrive at some acceptable response. Then a miracle occurred. It was as if the Holy Ghost had come upon me and I was resurrected from the dead. I looked straight into her eyes and said, "Transportation. My father is in transportation." At that moment the black man who had greeted me at the front entrance reappeared and announced that she had a phone call. It was almost as if this man knew my secret and was saving me from being humiliated.

Luckily, when she returned she had lost her train of thought and started a new line of interrogation.

"So where do you live?"

"In the Bronx," I answered.

"What part of the Bronx?"

I was dumbfounded. I remember thinking, what can I tell her? I live next to James Monroe High School? Would she even know where that was? I can't say the South Bronx. This would really shock her. Once again I was saved. Before I could even answer, Mrs. Lowenstein said to me, "You must live in Riverdale. Am I right?"

I had never been to Riverdale but I did know that it was the wealthiest community in the Bronx, and I did live near the Bronx River Parkway, so I sat there and lied.

"Yes. That's where I live," I said.

She continued to tell me what a beautiful place Riverdale was and how lucky I was to live there. I agreed.

After a brief stay that included listening to Barbara's mother play the piano and listening to Barbara talk to her friends on the phone about her glorious summer vacation, I announced that I was going home. Once again I found myself lying. This time the lie was about how I would get home. I said that my father was going to meet me at a particular location to drive me home. The truth was that I walked to the subway and took the Lexington Avenue subway home. As I got off the subway, I focused on the worn-down buildings in my neighborhood. While I walked up the five flights of broken-down and squeaky steps to my apartment, I reflected on the elevator operator in Barbara's building and the distinguished black man who greeted me at the door.

The day's visit was a portent of things to come. On my first day of school, I signed up for basketball and volleyball tryouts, in which I successfully competed. I was the only sophomore selected for both senior varsity teams. However, my adjustment in the classroom was not as easy. I quickly realized that the content and methodology used in teaching was quite different from what I was accustomed to in public school. In biology, we each had our own electronic microscope and were given a fetal pig to dissect, an occurrence usually restricted to college biology. In English, we were assigned a sonnet to write rather than given rexograph sheets to memorize. Furthermore, for each class we were given several books and were allowed to write in them, unlike in public school where few books were used and where writing in one's books was frowned upon because others would need to use them in the future. In spite of the challenging curriculum, I was able to compete and did quite well. Nevertheless, my success came while dodging criticism about my writing skills in English class, the nonstandard Spanish I spoke in Spanish class, and the funny way that I spoke in speech class.

Quite frankly, I could accept that my writing was not that of Hemingway and I understood that my speech was different from the rest of the students at Calhoun. But under no circumstances was I going to accept that my Spanish was any less correct than what was being spoken by a teacher who was not a native speaker. This invalidation of the Spanish spoken by Puerto Ricans has been a recurring issue in the lives of many young Puerto Rican students. The stupidity of teachers to accuse us of not speaking standard Spanish only shows their ignorance about linguistics. It is like saying that the English spoken in New York is not correct English. The implication for students who finally find a subject that they can achieve in, only to be met by criticism and negativity regarding who they are, is grave.

One additional obstacle that I faced was the small classes, which consisted of no more than fifteen students. In Catholic school, the class size was usually thirty-five to forty students. In James Monroe High School, classes were slightly smaller but still hovered around thirty. What the smaller classes forced me to do was to become an active class participant, a role that I did not welcome in a setting of which I did not feel a part.

Even more stressing than what I was facing in school was what was occurring out of school. The luncheons in restaurants with my teammates or classmates and the many weekend outings to ice skating parties, skiing trips, and shopping sprees to Saks and Lord & Taylor were just not activities that I could afford.

To admit that I was poor was to admit that I did not belong, a fact that no adolescent wishes to face. Therefore, I became a liar. It was easier for me to make up excuses for not participating in these out-of-school activities than to reveal who I was, namely a poor Puerto Rican kid from the South Bronx who would never be in their league. Moreover, my daily commute on the subway, while limousines lined up in front of the school and older students took cabs to the east side of Manhattan, served as reminders of our differences.

One day in school we received a flier from our brother school, McBurney. This was the same school mentioned in *Catcher in the Rye*. They were having a dance and were inviting all the girls from Calhoun to join them. I wanted to attend so badly, and my mother did everything in her power to help me get there.

She took some of her food money and gave me five dollars to buy a dress. I went to Alexander's on Third Avenue in the Bronx, and on the sales rack in the basement, I found the most beautiful wine-colored Empire dress. My father drove me to the dance, where we found ourselves stuck in traffic. Luckily for me, he left me a block away. I was close enough to walk and far enough so that no one would see his beat-up Rambler and the funny beret that made him look like Che Guevara.

The anticipation was intense. As I walked into the building and later into the room, I pretended to know where I was. I carried myself as if I had done this on many occasions. The beautiful room and the extremely cozy atmosphere of the dance impressed me. Unlike the dances conducted in James Monroe held in a large gym with lousy acoustics and no place to sit, this room had sofas scattered throughout the room and tables placed in different areas with punch and chips. I roamed around looking for someone I knew. Apparently, all the prep schools in Manhattan were invited, and the room was full of strangers.

Occasionally, I saw familiar faces and they would wave at me, but quickly turn their attention to their friends. It seemed that everyone knew each other. After a few hours of standing there and walking around the room, I found a public phone and called my father at my uncle's house. I asked him to please come and bring me home.

The day before Christmas vacation, I was emptying out my cubby and everyone around me was talking about what they were going to do for vacation. One was going to Aspen, the other to southern France, and another to the Caribbean. I was silent. Then the inquisition came.

"Where are you going, Alma?"

"Nowhere," I responded.

"How come?"

I stood there and for the first time I was completely ready to admit who I was.

"I am not going anywhere because my parents don't have the money to send me anywhere," I said. "That's why."

Silence overcame the room and each person quietly and quickly left. I guess no one had ever encountered a similar situation, and so the way to deal with it was to leave the premises. As the only remaining person, I quickly wiped the tears from my eyes and made a decision. I emptied all the contents from my cubby into a brown paper shopping bag and decided to return to James Monroe High School. As I left the school, which was located in a brownstone on the Upper West Side, I knew that this chapter in my life was closed forever.

There are times when I wonder what would have become of me if I had stayed at the Calhoun School. Nevertheless, any fantasies of richness or greatness are quickly overshadowed with the reality that any identity based on a lie eventually kills your spirit, and without that we are merely flesh.

I never told my parents about my decision not to return to the Calhoun School. I merely went back to James Monroe, where Miss Bass, the dean of girls, greeted me with open arms and quickly registered me for the following semester. One afternoon, my mother informed me that the head mistress from Calhoun had called and wanted to know where I was. I explained that I had decided to go to Monroe. My mother tried to convince me to reconsider my decision. I can remember her telling me of the great education that I was depriving myself of and the important contacts that I was going to make at Calhoun.

My father saw how emotionally upsetting the thought of going back to Calhoun was for me and decided to intervene. In a quiet but firm way, he looked at my mother and said, "*Dejala. Si no le gusta la escuela, no la debe de forsar*" (Leave her. If she doesn't like the school, you shouldn't force her).

For the first time, I really knew that my father understood exactly what I was going through. Maybe my maternal family's disapproval of him and their condescending attitude toward him gave him the insight to know what I was feeling.

To be an outsider is one thing, but to feel inferior because of factors out of your control is a feeling of complete powerlessness. It was not my fault that I was poor, but I was ashamed and guilty for not being like everyone at the Calhoun School. My father's approval of my choice as well as his validation of my feelings was worth whatever sorrow I had experienced at Calhoun. His compassion and sensitivity for me at this moment is something that I often think about and something that I hold very close to me. My father's stance was one that turned my life around and one that impacted on who I would become.

I often tell my students that I shared my room for the first sixteen years of my life with my sister Angie, or with someone who is a cross between Albert Einstein and Mother Teresa. Mind you, this is not an easy feat. When your only sibling is not far from perfect, your life can often become a nightmare, and mine is no exception. When Angie was not studying, she was praying for her salvation. For someone who never witnessed her doing anything sinful, the latter seemed to me to be senseless.

My rebelliousness, as well as my worldliness, stood in the way of my ever coming close to Angie's saintliness, and quite frankly, that was okay with me. I was more concerned about her obsessive studying than her praying, because I knew that I couldn't compete with her spirituality and how could you measure a person's state of grace anyway? There were times that her compassion for people and her goodness did stand in the way of my being seen in a favorable light, but I could live with this.

However, those straight As and her average, the highest in James Monroe High School for three years, were what I feared. The comparisons teachers would make between Angie and me were endless, and the damage was profound. Mrs. Laurie, my homeroom teacher in tenth grade, announced to the class while handing out report cards that I was not as smart as my older sister. Mr. Marcus, my math teacher, told my mother during open school day that I was not a serious student despite my superior performance on the algebra and geometry regents. I remember taking the geometry regents and scoring a 95 percent, only to be told that it was unfortunate that I did not get 100 percent like Angie.

The comparisons went on and on. One teacher referred to me as Angie the entire semester that he had me in his honors physics class, while others constantly expressed their disappointment that I was not the student she was. If Angie were just any honor student, the expectations of teachers would have been bearable, but she was not just any student. She was the highest performing one in a school that housed over three thousand students. This top ranking of hers turned my 90 percent grade point average into something that was of little value. My efforts went unnoticed and were interpreted as not being good enough.

In retrospect, these unwarranted and unjustly deserved comparisons and judgments about my academic abilities were quite detrimental in forming how I saw myself and in how I approach competitive situations. I can honestly say that my reluctance to compete, as well as the unrealistic and distorted perception of what is necessary to be considered worthy of acceptance in some domains, has contributed to determining what choices I have made in my life.

As one of only a few minorities in the Honor School at Monroe, I found refuge with Latino friends outside the Honor School and two Jewish friends who were high-achieving students but who were also outcasts in the Honor School. The two non-Latino friends were also considered outsiders, because one was a gay male and the other a female who had a mother who bordered on lunacy.

My peers provided me with the acceptance that I needed during an adolescence that was plagued with poverty, an overcrowded home, the eventual breakup of my parents, and the never-ending comparisons between me and my older sister. Among my Puerto Rican, Dominican, and Cuban friends, I was referred to as "the brain," because I was a member of the Honor School and in comparison to everyone else I was an outstanding student. This was a pleasant change from the incompetent image that my teachers had of me.

Some of these students, although not honor students, were on an academic track. However, many attended vocational schools or were in the general program at James Monroe. This was the program that we referred to as the Vietnam training program. It consisted of a watered-down curriculum that prepared you to do nothing. Many of these friends ended up in Vietnam, because they did not have college student status, a high draft number, or the money that would permit them to go to Canada and avoid the draft. Ironically, many had recently immigrated from Cuba, the Dominican Republic, and other

Latin American countries to a nation that they now found themselves defending in a war that they did not comprehend or know much about. Coincidentally, the late sixties was a time that had the greatest disproportionate representation of Hispanics in Vietnam than of any other group.

Not surprisingly, my fondest moments were spent with my friends who were not "honor students," but who were accepting of me. While I taught them math and proofread their papers, my friends taught me how to dance salsa, the facts of life, and how to be a normal teenager.

College and Beyond

Angie

I won several college scholarships, some even to Ivy League schools, but I followed my father's wishes and remained close to home. I commuted to Barnard, the women's college of Columbia University. My father felt that he could not afford the transportation to and from the colleges. Once again, I was the only Puerto Rican. This time, I had no confidence that I could hold my own against my sophisticated schoolmates. Despite the fact that I had always achieved academically, I felt that I had been admitted through the back door. I did not deserve to be admitted. I did not belong; I was not good enough. I was a token.

Many of the young Barnard women had attended New York City private schools, spent summers abroad, and had beautiful wardrobes. This was still the time that women wore stockings and dresses to school and men wore slacks or chinos, blazers and ties. It preceded the jeans, combat boots, and rebellious era we associate with the sixties. I remember attending several "teas" at Barnard, where there was a piano player who entertained us while we sedately sipped our tea and nibbled on dainty sandwiches. Several of my classmates wore chinchilla coats, which were the style back then. I had spent the summer working with kindergarten kids so I could buy material to sew dresses that I could wear to college.

For me, lunchtime at Barnard meant going to the Chock Full O' Nuts for a cream cheese on date nut bread sandwich or soup. I normally carried two subway tokens and a dollar or two for food. I recall being invited to go to lunch with some of my new classmates. We went to a Hungarian restaurant near the Columbia University campus. One glance at the *carte du jour* revealed that I could not afford anything. I feigned having a sudden stomachache and ordered tea and toast, which I consumed while my new friends ate what seemed, at the time, very exotic fare.

One of the first assignments in freshman composition was to read Shakespeare's *Measure for Measure*. I had considered myself fairly well read, because I had read many of Shakespeare's major plays, such as *Hamlet, Julius Caesar, Macbeth*, and *Romeo and Juliet*. I was very intimidated to see most of my classmates raise their hands when asked if they had read the assigned play. One student replied that she had not actually read *Measure for Measure*, but she had seen it performed by the Royal Shakespeare Company when she had last been to London. I kept thinking, what am I doing here?

It did not help any that there was a get-acquainted week when we had to introduce ourselves to each other. The women at my table decided to discuss what their fathers did for a living. One student's father was president of the American Medical Association; another's father was head of the physics department at Columbia. Again I thought, what am I doing here?

One student finally answered the question for me. When she found out that I was Puerto Rican, she was so stunned she blurted out, "Gee, you don't look Puerto Rican. You don't have an accent and you look white and clean! So that's why you are on scholarship. And all this time, I thought you were smart."

I never felt that I deserved to be at Barnard, so I dropped out and eloped before the end of the first semester. I was convinced that I was not college material anyway. Luckily, my first husband was a teacher and persuaded me to return to school. The following year, I started taking courses at his alma mater, The City College of New York. Many of my former high school classmates had already completed their first year when I arrived. This time, the college transition was much easier for me. The social adjustment was easier because it was familiar—students were from humble backgrounds like my own. I graduated summa cum laude, Phi Beta Kappa with a straight-A average in my major, psychology.

Despite my excellent academic background and my aspiration to go to graduate school, I hesitated to apply because of feelings of unworthiness. It was only at the insistence of a supervisor in the CCNY tutoring center where I worked part-time that I interviewed for an experimental program in guidance and counseling, which soon developed into a master's program. It was a federally funded program with the intention of training Puerto Rican guidance counselors sorely needed in the New York public school system.

It was unusual because numerous institutions in New York and Puerto Rico sponsored it. The Consortium for Bilingual Counselor Education joined together the University of Puerto Rico; the Inter-American University of Puerto Rico; the Catholic University of Ponce, Puerto Rico; and the City University of New York. There were two groups of students—one from the island and one from New York. The first summer was spent in New York and the following summer was spent in Puerto Rico. The New York group studied in New York during the academic year with mainly faculty from CUNY and the Puerto Rican group studied in Puerto Rico with faculty from the island. Both groups were united during the summers, and some faculty commuted back and forth.

Classes met five days a week, two of which were practicums at field sites where we had the opportunity to be mentored and engaged in related counseling activities. These field sites included colleges, community agencies, and high schools in New York and Puerto Rico where they would be assigned clients.

It was a positive experience for me. I was with all Puerto Rican students. We were a group of about thirty-five, and we got to know each other fairly well after a year and a half. The New York group consisted of twenty-three students. Small groups of students were placed under the supervision of Hispanic graduate faculty. The program was unusual on many counts. We were required to keep logs of our experiences, which we handed in to our supervisors. Many of these logs were published in a quarterly newsletter. We had access to the now defunct Guidance Laboratory of CUNY. We were able to use their videotaping facilities to simulate counseling sessions and then review and study them. We also had the opportunity to have the authors of the books we studied come to our groups and spend time with us. It was very exciting for me to be able to converse with these scholars. Most importantly, there were only pass/fail grades. This freed me to concentrate on learning rather than getting good grades. Once again, I became caught up in the joy of learning.

As I got older, the task of enduring the surprised reactions people had upon learning that I was Puerto Rican continued to distress me. My ability to fit in by not looking Puerto Rican or being seen as special or unusual filled me with great shame. Once again, being the accepted token was a double-edged sword.

Alma

For as long as I can remember, a college degree was something that I focused on achieving. This desire stemmed from various sources, including a way out of poverty and a sister who was such a high achiever that any chosen path remotely different for me would have been shameful. So in the name of saving face and escaping an adult life that would emulate that of my parents, I opted for a higher education. However, I never felt that my parents had the same goals for me. My mother felt that I should become a hairdresser or a secretary. I am not sure of my father's expectations, because he was quite disengaged from my life. I think that his goal was to get me through high school and the rest would be up to me.

After witnessing Angie's experience at Barnard and recalling my own at the Calhoun School, I knew that I would be attending one of the branches of the City University of New York. At the time, City College, Brooklyn College, and Hunter were the top three CUNY schools. I chose Hunter. It was the most accessible to public transportation and afforded me many job opportunities, which I took advantage of immediately after arriving at the college.

I managed to graduate from high school six months ahead of time and started Hunter College the following week on a cold day in January during New York's infamous garbage strike.

I remember coming home that first day only to find my father packing his belongings. In a tearful good-bye, he lectured me about how he was my father and how if I ever needed anything I could count on him.

Ironically, a few hours later my mother and I sat in the very same room in which my father and I had parted. She informed me that she only had thirty or forty dollars and felt that it would be best for me to drop out of school and start working. I quickly went to my pocketbook and counted $25 that I had saved to use for transportation for the rest of the semester. I remember her telling me that this was not going to be enough to get us through. She was expecting her first disability check, which was about $90 per month, and I was to receive $35 a month because I was a full-time student. But this was not enough for us to survive. There were rent, food, light, telephone, and many more things to think about. I remember sitting across from her in tears and telling her that this was so unfair. How could this be happening to me?

She merely listened and at one point even tried to convince me that being a secretary was a great career move. She told me that I was smart and would make a superior one. With luck I could become an administrative assistant. I told her that this was out of the question. There wasn't anything wrong with being a secretary, but this was the goal of the supposedly "less capable" students in my school. I was the academic student in the Honor School who graduated in the top five percent of her class. I was supposed to go to college. Why would I have taken all these science and math courses if I didn't need them?

The next day, I went to the financial aid office at Hunter. The counselor reviewed my financial situation and told me that she did not know how I was going to make it. I was told that it was impossible to survive with such little money. She advised me to drop out and return when I had enough money to go to school. I insisted on applying for loans, student work-study, grants, and anything else that they had. She reluctantly helped me and repeatedly shook her head while reciting the instructions and qualifications for financial aid.

That afternoon, I remembered that there was a dentist who worked in a dental clinic in the Bronx where I was employed on Saturdays who had told me that if I ever needed a job, he had a private practice on Park Avenue. I phoned him and luckily he was still looking for an assistant. I now had two dental assisting jobs and one job filing transcripts in the registrar's office. Now my challenge was to meet the demands of school, work, and attending to a mother who was not only sick but also heartbroken. Her marriage of twenty-three years had come to an end. She would sit for hours crying in the living room, and I would helplessly witness her sadness without knowing what to say or do.

During my first few semesters at Hunter, I lived a life with no room for anything but work, work, and more work. I took courses merely for the accumulation of credits. There was no time to enjoy or even contemplate nuances of the subject. I did what was required and knocked off course after course. Even if I had had the opportunity to have a social life, the fact that I was one of only three non-white students in my entering freshman class and the only one from the Bronx merely added to my dismal social life. Just as I was getting tired of a life lacking money and pleasure, and seriously contemplating dropping out of college, the Young Lords took over City College and student strikes multiplied throughout the various branches of the City University. The strikers were protesting for open admissions to the City University, the creation of ethnic studies, and a change of various school policies. Suddenly, I found myself an advocate and part of this movement that would transform my life and the world around me.

As the daughter of a left-wing socialist who advocated for the independence of Puerto Rico, and whose closest and dearest friends were part of its nationalist party, several of whom were still incarcerated and considered to be terrorists, my activism in the movement was a natural choice. For the first time in my life, the values instilled at home were being reinforced and advocated by my peers. Issues of unequal distribution of wealth and power, colonization, imperialism, capitalism, racism, and many more isms were familiar to me. What was different was that now a vast number of people were advocating such sentiments.

The institution of open admissions throughout the City University of New York transformed the complexion of all colleges. Hunter was transformed from a college with a predominantly white student population to one with a diverse population. I cherished this change, and in many ways my life was significantly impacted. The loneliness that I felt at Hunter was now replaced by friendships with people who were like me, namely, bicultural and marginalized in this society. It was not unusual for us to go out Friday night and dance salsa to the music of Willie Colon, Ray Barreto, and Eddie Palmeri, and then on Saturday groove on the music of Canned Heat or Santana at the Filmore East in the Village. We were flower children with a strong dose of salsa.

The institution of ethnic studies was the most important factor in engaging me in school. The few existing minority students prior to open admissions at Hunter College banded together to demand the inclusion of Black and Puerto Rican Studies. Once this demand was met, we made sure that these courses would have adequate enrollment by enrolling in them ourselves. For the first time in my life, both teachers and students were closer to what I was than what I was not. For the first time, I was being taught something about me and not about them. The emotion that I felt and still feel when I recollect this period in my life is like none that I have ever experienced. The validation of who I was had never occurred throughout my education. Even in Puerto Rico, I was seen as being from New York and virtually an outsider. Without a doubt, the student riots were the main vehicle in propelling me to finish my education, for now I found purpose and interest in what I was learning.

Part II

Critical Issues in Education

Chapter Six

Identity, Ethnicity, and Gender

Introduction

During the course of depicting our childhood experiences, a significant number of sociological, psychological, pedagogical, and developmental issues surfaced. These are forces that in one form or the other have influenced our education, our life choices, or our perspectives of both. To address all these variables would be beyond the purview of this work. Nonetheless, particular issues have emerged that we strongly feel teachers, counselors, and all professionals who work in schools, particularly with poor urban children of color, should examine. For this reason, they have been selected to be discussed.

Identity

We both recognize that while on the path to becoming who we are today, we often met with unexpected forces that influenced this journey. As two of a multitude of first-generation Nuyoricans, we were part of that age group that paved the way for subsequent immigrants of color. We were the ones who fought against being placed into traditional categories of race. We were the ones who refused to lose our language despite the consequences. We were the ones who embraced being referred to as "persons of color." We were also the ones who were often met with skepticism and criticism by those whom we expected to be accepting of us. However, we are also the ones who have worn and still feel the wounds inflicted by the many battles that we have fought. For this reason, we felt that a serious and open discussion about identity was warranted.

Identity can be understood as a fusion of personal and societal identity. Personal identity is the subjective sense of sameness and continuity that serves as a guide for one's life. Social identity includes one's roles, occupation, and gender identification, as well as religious, political, and philosophical ideologies.

The search for identity is most often thought of as the central task of adolescence. Perhaps the most cited theorist concerned with both identity and adolescence is Erik Erikson. In his theory of psychosocial development, he maintains that the adolescent must clarify who he is, what values he holds, and what he wants out of life. It is a difficult time in human development because adolescents are struggling to break from their parents, and at the same time find the appropriate friends, establish their sexual orientation, and set career goals for the future. In addition, they are solidifying their various political and religious ideologies. Failure to achieve an identity can lead to confusion and despair (1950, 68).

ETHNIC IDENTITY

For the youngster who is part of a racial or ethnic minority group, establishing an identity is even more complicated, because ethnicity and race are essential components of who they are and of the identity process. The minority individual must develop an ethnic/racial identity by coming to terms with his ethnic/racial membership as a salient reference group. But because identifying oneself as a member of a minority group can be painful if the group is the target of stereotyping and prejudice by the larger dominant society, this can lead to a poor self-concept. Moreover, it is also confusing because the minority member is often torn between two worlds with divergent and competing value systems.

This is particularly true of the Puerto Rican who has spent considerable time in New York and Puerto Rico. For those like us, who were part of the first and largest group of New York–born or –raised Puerto Ricans, issues of identity are complex. We are one of a few groups of immigrants to come to the United States in great numbers and who could not assimilate into what was a melting pot because of the color of our skin, the texture of our hair, or any other phenotypes used to exclude us. Our racial diversity created confusion in a system of racial classification that categorized persons as white or black (Rodriguez, 1991). This confusion, as well as our dual citizenship and close ties to the island of Puerto Rico, made us pioneers of what is now referred to as transnational identities, biculturality, cultural diversity, a cultural mosaic, and many of the nuances that have emerged in the past decades (Rodriguez, 1991). As pioneers of this transformation of the United States from a melting pot to a pluralistic society, we paved the way for other groups of color but without escaping considerable pain and a reinvention of what our identities were along the way.

Angie

There has been extensive work for almost two decades supporting ethnicity and race as essential components of the identity process for minorities. The resolution of this crisis can result in the minorities becoming alienated, assimilated, separated, or bicultural (Phinney, 1989, 1990; Phinney, Lochner, & Murphy, 1990).

Most of the effort in this sphere of inquiry has focused on the formulation of identity models, which explain the various stages through which minorities must pass to secure a positive ethnic or racial identity. Some models are meant to apply to minorities in general (Atkinson, Morten, & Sue, 1989; Atkinson, Thompson, & Grant, 1993; Phinney, 1989; Phinney & Alipuria, 1990; Phinney, Lochner, & Murphy, 1990; Phinney & Tarver, 1988). Other models have characterized the various stages of identity formation as they would apply to the development of identities for black, Asian, and Mexican Americans (Arce, 1981; Cross, 1991; Kim, 1981).

Although these general and specific models differ in terminologies and in the number of delineated stages, they share great similarities in the various phases through which the minority individual can go. Moreover, these models consider the forming of a positive racial/ethnic identity to be related to the establishment of the development of a healthy self-concept and further, that the nonacceptance of one's ethnic membership as a positive reference group can lead to self-estrangement and maladaptive behavior. There is some research to suggest that this is indeed the case. Phinney et al. (1990) concluded that the individual who does not explore and take a stand on issues regarding his status as a minority group member, or develop a secure ethnic identity, may be at risk for a poor self-concept.

Thus, the work on ethnic/racial identity formation suggests that unless one feels good about one's own racial/ethnic group, the appreciation of other groups may not be possible. You have to feel good about who you are in order to value others.

For both Alma and myself, the process of learning to know, accept, and like ourselves has been one that was inextricably linked with being Puerto Rican. Although there exists no specific model for the development of a Puerto Rican or Nuyorican identity, there are several similarities between the stages of existing models and our experiences.

For example, I feel that I have experienced all the possible resolutions of ethnic identity formation delineated by Phinney. I have felt alienated, marginalized, assimilated, withdrawn, and bicultural at different times in my life.

According to most of these models, the first phase that minorities go through is one where race and ethnicity are not salient in the individual's consciousness. Ethnicity is not an issue. This was true for both of us while we lived in the projects and attended St. Rita's. We were aware of differences in race, language, and ethnicity. We recognized that our family spoke Spanish and that we were different from our Irish and black neighbors, but that difference did not have a valence attached to it. We were not better or worse for being different.

The next characteristic stage is the conformity phase. During this stage, the minority person accepts the values of the dominant culture and may be at risk of internalizing negative stereotypes of his or her ethnic group and developing self-hatred. This was the case for me when the family moved out of the projects and attended St. Martin of Tours. Being Puerto Rican suddenly became a central characteristic and it carried a negative value. Having to commute to a school located in a community that did not welcome Hispanics and being faced with the prejudice and the insensitivity of teachers and students alike felt like an assault to my dignity and sense of self-worth. Unfortunately, as so many minorities do at this stage, I internalized negative stereotypes.

I became ashamed of what I looked like, where I lived, and who my parents were. I wanted to go unnoticed and blend in. I hated my abundant curly and frizzy hair. Why couldn't I have straight blonde hair? Why couldn't my home have Early American furniture instead of all that ethnic stuff like a Mexican serape and a Moroccan hassock? Or eat hot dogs instead of rice and beans? It was the first time that I was glad that my father did not participate in school activities. I was ashamed of his broken English, thick accent, and beret. Besides, I was concerned he might get emotionally worked up and say something inappropriate, such as calling J. Edgar Hoover a "son of a bitch" or saying something negative about the Pope.

The term *spic* was particularly painful. Puerto Ricans were hicks who were ignorant, loud, gaudy, and emotional. I remember my mixed feelings when asked to help translate for non-English-speaking Hispanics at school and elsewhere. One part of me wanted to be helpful and kind, but the other did not want, in the process of translating, to be identified as a *spic*.

A vivid scene that depicts my thinking during this stage remains etched in my mind. The archetypal Puerto Rican family is seated in the subway on their way to some location—probably a family get-together. The parents are dressed in clean and pressed clothing made of inexpensive synthetic fabrics that are shiny or very colorful. The little boys have navy blue suits of lightweight material with white shirts and clip-on bow ties. The little girls have lace or chiffon dresses that look like communion dresses except that they are in shades of shocking pink or some other very bright color. They are also wearing crisp petticoats so that the skirts of the dresses stick out. They usually have long hair with long banana curls. The shoes look like they are made of cardboard. Inevitably, the boys start fighting or fidgeting, and one of the parents yells in Spanish to stay still. The kids are tired of being still because the trip is long, perhaps from the Bronx to Brooklyn. They seem to command the attention of everyone in the subway car. This family definitely does not blend in. Sadly, I recall being embarrassed by these humble decent people. At the time, they looked so out of place in the subway. Sometimes they carried a gift for someone's birthday or a wedding. I would cringe.

On a particular day, I recall one such family who were obviously lost. They had gotten on the wrong train and needed help. They were arguing loudly in Spanish about where to get off and what to do. One member looked to see if they could find another Hispanic who could speak Spanish and direct them. All I could remember thinking was "Please, I hope they do not look at me." Luckily, they caught the attention of someone who did just that.

Academic achievement became a vehicle for my becoming socially acceptable. I desperately wanted to be seen as worthy and valuable in a society that saw my membership in a group as a sign of inferiority. I chose to identify with the role of academic achiever.

Typically, the next phase of identity formation is a transitional period characterized by dissonance. The person begins to question the pro-white attitudes and often has mixed feelings toward both the minority and the majority group. After I internalized many of the negative stereotypes of Puerto Ricans, we moved to the island of Puerto Rico. Strangely enough, on the island Alma and I were not considered to be Puerto Rican. We were called *gringas* or *las Americanas*. We were considered foreigners from New York. In fact, being seen as an American in Puerto Rico did not carry the significance I had anticipated. It was a confusing time for me. I was a spic in New York and a foreigner in Puerto Rico. I did not feel that I belonged to any group. This stage of confusion lasted a long time and most of it occurred unconsciously. It was akin to a cultural schizophrenia, if you will. It is only now as an adult that I can see more clearly that I straddled two different worlds with different value systems.

For example, generally speaking, American children are socialized to be self-sufficient, independent, and competitive. They are given a lot of praise for things they do on their own. They are separated from their mothers sooner than Puerto Rican children are. Many have their own rooms at a very early age. This and the many possessions that are theirs alone contribute to an earlier and stronger sense of self that is represented in the physical environment. They are encouraged to be verbally fluent by frequent verbal interaction with adults. These American child-rearing practices prepare the American child for school. There, he or she is not inhibited around adults and continues to seek their attention and approval by demonstrating acts of self-sufficiency.

The Puerto Rican child, on the other hand, is not encouraged to be so independent. He or she has more prolonged and frequent interaction with the mother than the American child. He or she is rarely left alone and rarely allowed sleepovers. The Puerto Rican child is encouraged to be respectful, obedient, well-mannered, clean, humble, and to have a sense of shame. Children are expected to defer to their elders and authority figures. Generally, the pattern of child-rearing is less permissive, the goal being obedience and conformity. It is not a matter of how well a child performs or the skill he acquires but to what extent he engages in socially accepted behavior (Irizarry, 1981). Puerto Rico has a more hierarchical social structure than the States. Women are more docile and protected. Girls are expected to be modest and demure. Men are more authoritarian. Boys are given more freedom. There is the machismo cult and the double standard.

We think that growing up in New York and being educated in an American educational system made us more aggressive, competitive, and self-sufficient than other Puerto Rican youngsters of our age and generation. Our father was very authoritarian, but he was absent. Our mother was actually quite permissive for a Latin mother. Although there was frequent and prolonged interaction with her and I felt especially attached to her, she allowed us considerable freedom. In any case, the family in Puerto Rico was scandalized at our behavior. The nature of the communication we engaged in with our mother shocked them. We never hesitated to give our opinions to her. We questioned her and were not at all submissive. Children were supposed to be seen and not heard. The family considered us disrespectful and arrogant, with few manners.

Ironically, in the States we were considered very respectful and obedient and I was often the teacher's pet. In the States, I was frequently taunted as a crybaby. I wished that I could be less sensitive and emotional. I spent years trying to control and repress my emotions and be more stoic and rational. In high school in Puerto Rico, I felt more at home to express my feelings. By the time I was a graduate student in the Consortium, I had achieved more control and was actually seen by my Puerto Rican peers as aloof.

In general, the educational experience in Puerto Rico was very positive for both of us. I experienced that learning could be fun once again. My acceptance by teachers and fellow classmates was dependent on who I was rather than on how I could perform. I felt respected and accepted. I was relaxed and felt no compunction to prove myself to anyone. American nuns ran the Catholic high school

I attended. Their attempts to impose their values on the class did not always succeed. At one point, one of these American teachers tried to motivate the class by seating students according to their grade point average. The student with the highest grade point average sat in the first seat in the first row. The student with the lowest grade point average sat in the last seat in the last row. The student with the lowest grade point average became a kind of celebrity in the class. The rest of his classmates kidded him and he took it good-naturedly. I am not quite sure if the students rallied around him out of defiance at the indignity they felt he had to endure. Perhaps it can be explained again by the difference in values.

Dignidad, one's personal worth (as distinct from one's position in the social structure) is highly valued in Puerto Rico. One can also refer to *personalismo,* the uniqueness and individuality of each human being. In this instance, the young man was unique in his ability to be the greatest underachiever in class. This result was not what the teacher expected. This is an example of a culture clash. Although it was a very confusing time for me, I was able to learn that the American value system was not the definitive standard.

Returning to New York fourteen months later was again, in some ways, a culture shock. Once again, my self-esteem was threatened. Once again, my identity became dependent on my academic achievement. I became the exception or token for the non-Hispanics and the activist for the Puerto Ricans. I felt great pressure in having to represent my ethnic group. I was often asked questions that I was expected to answer for all Puerto Ricans. "How do Puerto Ricans feel about the Vietnam War?" It was difficult enough articulating how I felt about the war, let alone trying to answer for my entire ethnic group. Who was I—a New Yorker, an American, a white female, a person of color, a Puerto Rican, a Nuyorican?

As much as I enjoyed my educational experience in Puerto Rico, I did not feel like a Puerto Rican. My interaction with my mother's family left a bitter taste in my mouth. Their racism and class-consciousness was something I did not want to identify with. But it was no better in the continental United States. Here was a heterogeneous society that articulated assimilation and that differences should not exist but in fact tolerated and supported separate schools, jobs, and housing for those who were racially and ethnically different. My generation witnessed the civil rights movement and the assassination of Dr. Martin Luther King Jr. I did not identify with white America.

On the other hand, women fared better in the American system. There was less of a double standard and a fairer division of labor. Latina women had to endure so much machismo and inferior status from their men. During the time I was getting my master's degree, I was married to a non-Hispanic. I was criticized by my own ethnic group for marrying a white man. Marrying a white man was akin to collaborating with the enemy. Not choosing a Latino man was seen as a political statement.

I experienced a very clear identity crisis. The time I spent in Puerto Rico afforded me the opportunity to experience both cultures up close. I saw the positive and the negative side of each group. That is why I do not identify with the next stage, which is typically described in the models of ethnic and racial identity formation as a resistance stage. The individual characteristically embraces his or her own group unquestionably and rejects the dominant values. The person accepts racism and oppression as a reality in his or her life. The minority individual often develops a negative attitude toward whites. The stage can also be distinguished by anger, outrage, guilt, embarrassment, and self-directed anger because of the former desire to be white. It is distinguished by a *we* versus *them* mentality.

Most likely this resistance stage did not occur for me because my Puerto Rican identity was short-lived. Instead, when we returned to New York after the fourteen months in Puerto Rico, I adopted a Nuyorican identity. This consisted of identifying myself as a person of Puerto Rican heritage and culture who was born in New York and was English-dominant and a person of color. I felt a connection and commonality of experience with American blacks brought up in New York, which many Puerto Ricans from the island cannot comprehend. In the United States, race is dichotomized; you are either white or nonwhite. Puerto Ricans, being a racially mixed group, are identified as nonwhite. As long as I could remember, I have been identified as a nonwhite New Yorker. I shared this identity with blacks from New York.

What I do remember experiencing, which is part of this stage, is embarrassment and self-directed anger at wanting to be white. These feelings were not confined to only one stage in my life.

Although I believe that racism is a major worldwide problem, I also do not believe that *all* whites are racists. I believe that most people have some form of prejudice because of being socialized in America. Perhaps my beliefs come from my marriage at an early age to a white man who was not a racist. My second marriage was to an African born in Europe. I have been married to a white and a black man and feel that I have been exposed to many nationalities, races, and traditions.

The closest I have felt to a *we* versus *them* mentality was working for an equal opportunity program at the City University of New York. I joined the SEEK Program (Search for Education Elevation and Knowledge) in the early 1970s as a counselor. Today, I run the program at Baruch College. The SEEK Program was designed to open the door to higher education for students from New York City who had neither the strong academic background nor the economic resources to pursue a college education. It was created by the New York black and Latino state legislators in 1966 with the objective of giving black and Latino youngsters an opportunity to go to college. Not only were most of the SEEK students black or Hispanic, but most of the staff and faculty employed in the program were and are still black or Hispanic. In those early days, many of the Baruch faculty were against having such a program at the college because they felt that it would lower the standards of the institution. Many felt that the counselors and staff of the program were not qualified, and thus for over two decades they were not embraced as legitimate members of the Baruch community. This bonded the SEEK people and created an isolation and segregation that lasted for many years. During that period, SEEK functioned as a separate entity within the institution. Once again, I felt like an outsider and a second-class citizen.

The bonding with people of color and having a Nuyorican identity did not mean that I accepted wholeheartedly that the SEEK staff could do no wrong. I often differed with colleagues with regard to philosophy and methodology. I was often seen as conservative or "white" in my thinking. Many of the New York Puerto

Ricans reproached me for marrying outside of my group. What I feel about being Nuyorican is pride. I appreciate and continue to honor the beauty, tenacity, and music, even Spanglish, of my group. Nevertheless, I feel like a citizen of the world, and more importantly, a spiritual being going through a human experience.

Alma

While the proposed model of identity formation that Angie presents is much needed in understanding the evolutionary process of identity, in particular of persons of color, it examines this phenomenon from a psychological perspective, which does not explain the historical and social components of identity. The identity formation of the first generation of Puerto Ricans born and raised in New York was a process that was unlike that of any prior immigrant group. This generation faced issues of race that other groups had never before confronted. Prior to our arrival in New York, persons were categorized as either Caucasian or Negroid. The racial diversity of the Puerto Rican population contributed to the reconsideration of how race is defined in this nation, particularly in New York. While this reconsideration has contributed to a reformulation of how we see race in this nation, it is without a doubt what caused much pain for our generation. Children with birth certificates that classified us as white grew up to find out that they in fact were not considered or treated as such. In other instances, children classified as Negro had brothers and sisters who were classified as white. To add to the problem, race in Puerto Rico was categorized according to phenotypes or racial characteristics, resulting in greater confusion. The close ties to the island as well as American citizenship—a political status shared by all Puerto Ricans—contributed even more to the complexity of this matter. In one place you were considered a Negro, while in another you were judged on the texture of your hair, or your facial features.

For both of us the perplexity became greater when our grandmother used her own idiosyncratic categorization of race, which was confounded with issues of class. In this case, we found ourselves two sisters with white European features being classified as "persons of color" in Puerto Rico by a grandmother who was racist and elitist, while in New York we were repeatedly told that we should identify ourselves as Spanish and not Puerto Rican. This we were told by people who thought they were doing us a favor by providing us with such advice. Added to this was the fact that our father was active in the Puerto Rican Nationalist Movement and my mother was very proud of being Puerto Rican.

Furthermore, our being categorized in New York as Puerto Rican rather than American, only to be considered *Americana* in Puerto Rico, continued to add greater volume to the never-ending maze of which we as children and young adults found ourselves a part.

My identity process did follow many of the same steps that Angie's model presents, namely, recognition that I was different from the majority population, hating the fact that I was different, and then coming to terms with who I ultimately accepted myself as being. Nonetheless, the fact that such a process was as painful and at times as destructive as it was is evidence of the magnitude of nonpsychological variables that impacted on the final psychological process of identity formation.

Identity in the projects was not an issue, partly because of the racial composition of the community, but also to some extent because of our age.

Once we left the projects, as Angie explains, came the period when I began to consider who I was as something to separate myself from. As absurd or impossible as it might sound, this was the message that was being sent to me—namely, become someone else. Although there were times that I did aspire to being Irish because of the favorable status of being Irish in a Catholic school, and did feel shame because I was Puerto Rican, these feelings of self-hate were quickly overshadowed by the sobering reality that I was who I was.

My response to the negative response was to find comfort with those who were like me. The negative value associated with being Puerto Rican was not something that I agreed with (although I admit to the internalization of this negativity) or chose; it was something that was bestowed upon me. In the same way that I responded to the racism at St. Martin of Tours, I responded to my grandmother's racist and exclusionary ways. I found consolation among persons like myself, classmates who had also migrated to Puerto Rico from New York, and I developed my new identity, namely, that of a Nuyorican or someone who is a Puerto Rican from New York. This is also a way of not allowing people to classify me. In essence, it is a way to categorize myself rather than allow other people to fit me into whatever categories they feel a need to place me.

This identity allowed me to label myself in ways that talked to my experience in a large city with intense poverty, cold winters, substandard housing, racism, at times inept teachers, crime, isolation, exclusion, and feelings of being different. I am not white or black, I am not an *Americana* but I am an *Americana*, and I am usually the one and only or the one of a few, translated into feelings of just not belonging. Once again, the path I took was one of finding comfort with those who shared a common experience, namely, Nuyoricans.

Nonetheless, while this identity does represent who I am, it is one that is fluid and transforms into one of a Puerto Rican when politically and socially necessary. An attack on Puerto Ricans is an attack on me, and when counting Puerto Ricans, count me in. Nonetheless, when deep sentiments arise about what makes me cry, laugh, love, and hate, my Nuyorican-ness is rightfully and strongly present.

SUMMARY

For the most part, the educational process that we experienced did not support the development of a positive ethnic/racial identity. There were few role models available for us to identify with. There was no curriculum that included our history.

GENDER IDENTITY

Angie

My mother was the greatest influence on the formation of my identity as a woman. What I have felt about the roles of wife and mother has been shaped by my reactions to how she accepted and carried out her female roles.

In hindsight I see her now as very strong, but for a large part of my childhood I saw my mother as helpless, weak, and dependent. I saw her as a victim and a martyr.

My mother was very loving, nurturing, and affectionate. Her hugs and kisses were so frequent and intense that I would feel overwhelmed and at times had to pull away from her. She was my first teacher and friend. I relied on her for everything. I remember feeling terrified at the thought that she could die and I would be left without her.

She often expressed that she was able to deal with the many disappointments in her life and the unhappiness of her marriage by the joy of being my mother. I often heard the story of her gaining back much of her health when she became pregnant with me. She had complete faith in me and was my greatest fan. I saw her as smart, capable, and wise.

Around the fourth grade (nine years old), I began to feel that I was responsible for my mother's well-being and happiness. At that time, our roles started to shift and I became the caretaker and confidante. In comparison to the other women in the projects, my mother had more freedom and control of her life. She appeared to be strong and capable to those around her. But I was privy to her disillusionment with her marriage and her unhappiness and loneliness.

From her, I learned that my father spent his evenings seeking pleasure and entertainment with other women and friends. She often had me go through his pockets. I found theater, nightclub, cabaret, and movie ticket stubs. I even found an earring once. He was living a separate and exciting life. She could not join him in his adventures because someone had to take care of the children, and she made the choice to meet her responsibilities. Rather than argue and be resentful about it, she felt that being a mother was the most righteous calling. My father wanted a playmate and partner who shared his love of adventure.

In my head, I felt that mom chose us instead of my father. She sacrificed her relationship with my father to honor her commitment of being a good parent. She sacrificed excitement and adventure to be my mother and she did it nobly, stoically. She had had a very wonderful life as a single woman before her illness. She had been a fun-loving and lighthearted person. But life had not been fair or kind to her. She was the victim of a chronic and debilitating disease. She married a man who did not appreciate or honor her. But marriage to him produced the most important thing in her life—her children. Thus, she accepted her fate, even embraced it. I often asked her why she did not leave my father. She stayed because he provided economically for us and having a husband, even an absent one, offered for us some measure of protection. The fourth grade coincided with the height of religious indoctrination, and I saw my mother as the good, virtuous one. She was able to sacrifice for love as the martyrs had done. My father was the selfish adulterer and sinner. In the cold war between my parents, I was my mother's ally and greatest defender.

I did everything I could to make my mother's life easier. Because she trusted me so much, I became very trustworthy—the self-fulfilling prophecy. The more my mother relied on me, the more reliable I became. I tried to please her because it made her so happy. This also meant being able to make sacrifices for her even if they were small ones. I remember her wanting to buy me a pocketbook at Woolworth's as a birthday gift one year. I did not like it but she was so insistent about its attractiveness that I agreed. I never used it, but it made her so happy that I went along with it. I do not ever remember actually ever saying "no" to my mother during my childhood. I accommodated my needs to hers. I also took on many of the roles generally left to the husband in a family.

When my mother was able to return to work, thus eliminating our economic dependence on my father, I encouraged my mother to stand up for herself. If he made her so unhappy and he was rarely around anyway, why stay married to him? She was capable of taking care of herself and us. After the serious physical and verbal confrontation I had with my father, my mother decided to move us to Puerto Rico. Unfortunately, she became ill once again and we had to return to live with my father. During our stay in Puerto Rico, I suffered tremendous guilt for having advised her to leave my father. Every time we faced another obstacle like hunger, discrimination, or humiliation, I felt responsible for the suffering we were undergoing. I had been wrong. She was not strong enough to live by herself.

In summary, from my mother I got the following notions:

1. Women are more responsible than men.
2. Men have more freedom than women.
3. Men have more fun than women.
4. Motherhood is akin to sainthood.
5. Mothers are expected to make sacrifices.
6. Motherhood is the most important role for a woman.
7. An educated woman has more choices.
8. Women are not as strong as men.

Latina Identity

I saw my mother as living a life in which she was stuck. But in comparison to the Latina women around her, she lived a charmed life. Many of these women were victims of violence and physical abuse. The men in their lives dominated them. They had the last say. Women waited on their men hand and foot. In some ways it was a blessing that my father was so absent, because some women had husbands who did not allow them to cross the street to buy groceries. They were prisoners in their own homes.

Similarly, Latina girls of our age group were very overprotected. They were not allowed to do what Alma and I did regularly: skate, ride bikes, and spend hours in the playground. They stayed at home and were expected to help with cooking and cleaning. We helped at home but were given much freedom.

This was the case for the behavior expected of girls in Puerto Rico. We shocked our relatives by our assertive behavior. I reasoned that if women had it harder than men, then Latinas who were married to Latinos were really in trouble.

Chapter Seven

Community

Recognizing the makeup of a community is vital in understanding the experiences that children confront both in and out of the classroom. Its structure as well as its composition will ultimately affect their development (Agueros, 1991; Darling-Hammond, 1997; hooks, 1994; Kozol, 1992; Kozol, 1995; Ladson-Billings, 1994; Macedo, 1996).

Where you live, who teaches you, who your fellow classmates are, and whether you are a member of that community or an outsider will, undoubtedly, mold the climate of the classroom. In essence, your status in a school community will play a significant role in the quality of that experience and in some instances will determine your success or failure in school. Our combined experiences—which include attending public schools, Catholic schools, private independent schools, private colleges, and public institutions of higher learning, as well as being educated in New York City and in Puerto Rico—attest to the fact that who you are and your status within that community can and does affect how you are perceived by those who have your future in their hands. This will ultimately contribute to how you see yourself.

School is a microcosm of society, and a child's status within that society, more specifically within that local community, will have an impact on his or her education. In inner cities it is no secret that the highest performing schools are usually located in affluent white areas. Often, well-intentioned parents such as ours move children from one neighborhood to another in hopes of improving that child's education, without realizing that the child's self-image is being compromised in the name of "a better neighborhood" or a "better school." Prior to school, parents are the principal agents in the formation of the child's self-concept. Once that child starts school, the teacher and his or her classmates become increasingly important in determining how that child will feel about himself/herself, which will ultimately be reflected in the child's attitude regarding the education domain. If the child perceives himself/herself as not capable of succeeding, his or her desire to even attempt to succeed in such an environment will be hampered. Our hats are off to all those children who find themselves in similar situations who cannot articulate what is happening to them but continue to try and succeed in such an environment. They are the ones who silently carry the scars inflicted at a young age by a system that can often be unkind and unwelcoming.

Furthermore, the creation and implementation of educational policy is also very often carried out without such considerations. The academic benefits of having children bussed from one district to another for whatever reason is at times overshadowed by the disruption in the child's life. This is not to say that children cannot benefit from programs outside their local school. However, in order for the child to benefit from the experience, teachers must be cognizant of these social dynamics.

Our status has changed throughout the course of our education, depending on who was teaching us, the location of the school, and the population being taught. Our experience at St. Rita's School, for example, while living in the projects was one of participation and engagement. Community and school were closely connected. Our lives revolved around school and around the major events such as baptism, communion, confirmation, graduation, Sunday mass, and weddings. Furthermore, my mother's function as the principal's secretary, a job that she did in exchange for free tuition, further added to our engagement with school and strengthened the relationship between parental participation, community, and school.

The demographics of the school contributed to this engagement. Although the population of the community was predominantly people of color, the school's demographics reflected pretty much equal representation of whites, blacks, and Puerto Ricans. The equalization of races resulted in no one dominant or preferred group. Although one could not escape the higher status of being Irish in an environment dominated by Irish nuns and priests, there was never a feeling that we did not belong or that this institution was not ours.

We all recognized St. Rita's as ours, and the nuns and priests recognized the importance of each one of us in the survival of this rundown school with broken bathrooms, poor lighting, squeaky floors, substandard heating, and overcrowded classrooms. Nonetheless, the physical condition of St. Rita's did not stand in the way of educating children who came from poor homes with parents who usually had very little formal education and who were more often than not immigrants or southern blacks who were new to a large urban city. This recognition of our similarities played out in the classroom, where we were all expected to learn and thus judged by the same standards.

Once we left the projects and lived in a neighborhood that necessitated our taking public transportation to school, our status changed. Not only were we outsiders, but our ethnicity in a predominantly Irish and Italian neighborhood gave credence to the notion of our not belonging. In a city where Puerto Ricans were concentrated in few ethnic enclaves throughout its boroughs, our presence in a predominantly white neighborhood was often met with fear and unflattering stereotypes. We were looked upon as uneducated hicks, also known as "spics," with pointed shoes, who were gang members and welfare recipients and who spoke very little English. We were also considered to be violent, explosive, and dangerous.

This was a time in which the largest migration of Puerto Ricans to the United States had recently occurred. The fact that our settlement patterns were concentrated in a few selected areas of the South Bronx, Manhattan, and Brooklyn contributed to furthering the misconceptions of who we were, because any knowledge about us came from the media, which usually depicted Puerto Ricans being arrested or in other negative situations. This was a time when television came into our homes and transformed our lives in unimaginable ways; it became progressively more important in informing us about the world (Steinberg & Kincheloe, 1997). The absence of Puerto Ricans in the media helped to perpetuate notions of our marginality in American society, while movies such as *West Side Story* did little to dispel unflattering stereotypes.

Ironically, the isolation and insulation of our communities in the projects and in other similar ghettos, which provided us with security and a feeling of belonging, conversely contributed to our being stereotyped and to separating us from the mainstream. We became marginalized people in what we thought was a "melting pot." These negative images of who we were played out in the classroom. For several years, I sat in the back of the room with the other three Puerto Ricans. I can't remember once ever having a conversation with any of my teachers.

Although the physical conditions of the school were far superior to those found in St. Rita's, the emotional bond was not there, resulting in my perception of school as something that I had to attend, not something that I felt a part of.

In Puerto Rico, our substandard Spanish skills became linguistic markers of our not being from the island. Nevertheless, we were accepted by our peers and eventually became integral members of our classes. Nonetheless, we were still seen as *las Americanas* or *las gringas*, and thus distinguished from the majority of the population.

In high school, where we lived did not play a major role in our school experience. The school community was a microcosm of the larger community, with the predominantly white Honor School viewed as the elite group. Students who were a part of the most diverse population of the school, the nonhonors academic programs, were a tier below the honor students. The next and lowest tier of students were those in commercial and general academic tracks. This segment was made up predominantly of blacks and Latinos, and because of the track they were on, they would end up with the lower-paying jobs. As members of the Honor School, we were part of the elite of that community, and the few of us who were Latino or black were seen as "the exceptions." The effects of this labeling and its implications about the other members of our group had a great influence on how we perceived ourselves and on our social dynamics.

Chapter Eight

Language

Examination of the linguistic patterns of past immigrant groups in the United States shows that by the third generation, complete linguistic acculturation has occurred. That is, the immigrant language is replaced by the exclusive use of English. Traditionally, the first generation is characterized by the use of the ethnic mother tongue at home, followed by the use of both English and the immigrant tongue by the second generation, and then by the exclusive use of English by members of the third generation. In some cases, this shift occurs within one generation (Rubal-Lopez, 1992).

But there is evidence to show that the linguistic behavior of Puerto Ricans in the United States does not follow this pattern. Unlike past immigrant groups, Puerto Ricans are maintaining their ethnic language while simultaneously using English in their linguistic repertoire. The unusual linguistic patterns of Puerto Ricans have prompted interest from many researchers in various fields of study (Flores, Attinasi, & Pedraza, 1981; Zentella, 1997).

The decision to maintain our language, in the same way as our stance on race—which opposed our being dichotomized as black or white—is still another example of how the Nuyorican has been able to adapt to living in two worlds. Our close ties to the island as well as our constricted living conditions in ethnic enclaves have all contributed to the maintenance of Spanish in New York.

The importance of knowing English was something that we knew at a very young age. Our father, despite his wealth of knowledge in many subjects, always worked in low-paying jobs because of his lack of oral skills. His search for knowledge moved him to read the newspapers in English. However, his spoken language was and still is very difficult to comprehend.

The power of language and its role in determining one's status in American society were well understood by both our parents. Nonetheless, each had their own perspective about English and the role that it should play in the lives of their two girls.

My father, who was involved with the nationalist movement of Puerto Rico and was as anti-American as you could be without being a terrorist, refused to speak English in the home. He feared having children who did not speak Spanish. His stance on speaking Spanish at home was based on ideological reasons, while my mother's choice to speak English at home was based on social mobility and her need to protect us. My mother was very aware of the codes of power that are played out in school and the disadvantages that a child has if he does not possess this code (Delpit, 1995).

She witnessed the very difficult time that Angie had because she only spoke in Spanish when she first entered school, so she decided to speak to us in English. My mother's education, which consisted of a high school education in Puerto Rico during a time when the island's language policy dictated the use of English in school, provided her with that option. Needless to say, this choice was not available to many of my friends' parents, who spoke only Spanish.

Our home's linguistic repertoire consisted of both my parents speaking in two different languages when addressing us, the use of Spanish when speaking to one another and our code switching when speaking to both of them.

Both approaches have had their impact on our lives. The use of English at home did provide us with the linguistic code necessary for academic achievement. This was an advantage that many of our Spanish-dominant friends who had monolingual parents with less education did not have. Our English competency has allowed us to compete and succeed in academic and professional environments oftentimes restricted to those who have been privy to this code. We have not suffered the shame and negative consequences of being labeled "limited English proficient," "uneducable," "stupid," or any of the many harmful and derogatory categories reserved for those who do not speak English. In fact, our success as students as well as professionals in the workplace has very often been interpreted as stemming from various sources while overlooking what may be the most important, namely, our knowledge of the dominant language. We have at times been revered as persons who are the exception, when possibly language might be the underlying factor in our success.

On the other hand, our spoken Spanish has never reached native competency. While we can carry on a conversation and function in any Spanish-speaking environment, English is the language that we feel most comfortable with when writing and performing any kind of academic work or official function. Our apparent dominance in English has led to criticism by those who perceive this as "trying to be *Americana*," while there are still those who must let us know when speaking Spanish that our pronunciation or usage is not that of a native speaker. Our mixture of Spanish and English, also referred to as Spanglish, is seen as an inferior code. The lack of proficiency in Spanish at the level of native speakers has been a marker for our not being "true Puerto Ricans" and our subsequent exclusion from certain circles reserved for such individuals. The irony of this is that those engaged in the labeling have often been Puerto Ricans who are in pursuit of maintaining their language and culture, but who have often dealt with the "Nuyorican" in a prejudicial, exclusionary, and elitist manner and have unwittingly become the oppressor. Our experiences were those of marginalized persons who were living in two worlds (Stonequist, 1961; Villanueva, 1993; Zentella, 1997).

To further complicate matters, native Puerto Ricans are constantly being criticized for how they speak Spanish. There are certain groups within the Spanish-speaking world that pride themselves on having the monopoly on speaking "correct Spanish." What these ignorant people do not know is that we all speak a variety of one language or another and it is not about one form being better or worse. It is about being understood. Teachers, in particular Spanish teachers who have been taught by such linguistic elitists in college, continue to promulgate this lie about the inferiority of Puerto Rican Spanish. What they don't say is that La Academia Real has recognized Puerto Rican Spanish as one of the varieties of Spanish that they find acceptable.

Chapter Nine

Class, Home, Values, and School

In the field of education, the role of economic class and its impact on academic achievement, behavior in the classroom, school dropout rates, college enrollment, literacy rates, and such measures of school success are repeatedly used to explain the lack of academic achievement of poor children.

In study after study, class is presented as the common thread to understanding or rationalizing why our children are failing. Student teachers are exposed to an education that relies on name-calling, using labels such as "disadvantaged," "at-risk," "learning disabled," and "the underclass" to explain its failures. The research supporting the use of these labels informs educators about how school achievement is intimately and inevitably linked with socioeconomic status (Delpit, 1995). There is substantial documented evidence of effective schools in which poor children have shown academic achievement equal to that of their middle-class peers (Edmonds, 1986). However, this is overlooked and our youth are presented as failures rather than as victims of unsuccessful institutions. What is not considered is how this variable of socioeconomic status is defined or measured.

For example, in New York public schools, the categorization of a school's population is very often measured by the percent of free lunches in that school. The problem with such a measure is that it places everyone into the "below poverty" category without considering inaccurate accounts of income reported by parents in order to get these free lunches, and it disregards other variables that might be more accurate for predicting academic success. Such research leads down a dead-end path, resulting in inaccurate reports of the relationship of one's economic well-being with one's school performance.

For children of immigrants, inquiries about why they succeed or fail in school are often shallow and explain very little (Nieto, 1997). The great range and diversity of class, education, socioeconomic level as well as occupation prior to migration, country of origin, date of arrival, language or languages spoken at home, and one's race are often overshadowed by broad categories of race or ethnicity. With immigrant populations of people of color, such assumptions are detrimental and lead to inaccurate conclusions about them. Puerto Ricans, for example, as well as Dominicans, Cubans, Colombians, and Mexicans, are often labeled "Hispanic" without considering any of the above criteria. Even more importantly, the reasons surrounding their immigration, facts that can provide a better understanding of their attitudes and behaviors, are often overlooked.

The dichotomy between the values of the poor and those of the middle class when speaking of academic success is another example of a broad stroke used for all that can often be imprecise and misleading. Often, behaviors are attributed to values without taking into account that one might engage in a behavior because of a lack of resources rather than because of values.

For example, if you ask immigrants who have recently arrived to the United States the reasons surrounding their immigration, they most likely will talk about a desire to provide an education for their children. Nonetheless, many do not understand or know how to safeguard their children's success in such a domain. In this case, the value placed on educating their children is overshadowed by a lack of information regarding how to realize their goals. Oftentimes, erroneous assumptions about a lack of values are made when what should be addressed is the lack of knowledge or resources available to the person in question. The lack of values argument repeatedly presents the poor as having none or lower values than the middle class, which is portrayed as one that places a value on education.

Furthermore, immigrant parents do not necessarily have values that are incompatible with the school. What they do not have is a command of the English language to assist their child, or the knowledge of where to find appropriate help. The issue is one of means, not values. In comparison, other immigrant parents with similar origins, the same length of time in the United States, and the same education, but with a greater number of family members already living in the United States, have an advantage over immigrants who find themselves alone in such a situation.

Alma's first childhood memories were not of poverty, suffering, or any of the great evils or images that are associated with projects. This is not to say that we were not poor. We lived in public housing, lived in tenements, and suffered the daily indignities associated with being poor in a society that places the blame for such an existence on those living in such conditions. Nonetheless, our lives, although very similar, were also very different in some ways from some of those living beside us, and this difference cannot be measured in terms of money. In this case, class takes precedence. How my parents viewed life, in particular education and knowledge, is key to understanding the diversity within poor populations and the danger of dumping persons into categories and making generalizations about them.

Any substantive discussion of class must address not only materiality, but also behaviors and attitudes (hooks, 1994). Throughout our lives, class has been a mediating factor, not only in how we saw life, but also in the ways that we were seen and are still seen. Recently, a friend of Alma's who rightfully prides herself on attaining a master's degree and having a fruitful life after years of foster placement, drug use, physical abuse, and dire poverty, was discussing where she lived in the Bronx while she attended college. When Alma told her that we had lived in that same neighborhood, she responded that how lucky we were to have been able to move out before it became a crime-infested ghetto. The reality is that we lived in that area six months before she moved there. As victims of a robbery and attempted rape, our mother and Alma chose, respectively, to move to a safer area.

When issues of poverty surface in their conversations, this person, whom Alma has known for many years (but whom she met as an adult), repeatedly tries to classify Alma as someone who was in a better financial situation than she was. She attributes the fact that Alma is a faculty member and has a doctorate to her privileged life.

She has often reminded Alma that her own life choices would have probably been different and better had she had a more economically privileged childhood. After many years of explaining to her that she, too, was a victim of poverty, Alma now allows her to rationalize the differences in their lives in whatever way she chooses.

As Alma says, she does not want to get into a conversation about who is the "poorer Puerto Rican." It makes no sense.

What this person does not know is that throughout our childhood, we were financially poorer than most of our friends because of choices that our parents made about our lives. This became apparent when we left the projects and had friends who lived in their own private houses or resided in cleaner and better-kept buildings. In high school, this was even more evident in the quality of clothes that they wore, the private homes that they owned, and in the Sweet Sixteen parties that they had, things that we never could afford. Moreover, many of these same friends chose not to continue with their education after high school in spite of the fact that their parents could have facilitated such a choice. Many are still more affluent than we are, and not surprisingly have children who have also chosen not to further their education after high school.

Alma's friend has mistakenly attributed Alma's life choices to her economic resources rather than to choices and attitudes that she derived from her home. For this reason, when we address issues of class we inevitably must talk about home. If there was one thing that distinguished us from many of our childhood friends, it was the knowledge that there was a world beyond the neighborhood. Our eccentric father introduced knowledge about a world outside our immediate universe to us, and the knowledge of how to carve a niche in it was taught by our practical mom.

While many of our friends' parents chose to invest their hard-earned money on furniture or for a down payment on a home, our father chose to always have a car, a necessary item of transportation since he worked in the airplane industry in Westbury, Long Island. It was usually a jalopy that my father was constantly repairing, but this choice allowed us to see a world that many of our friends as children never got to see. It is not an exaggeration to say that some of our friends never saw a beach, or visited the sights of Manhattan, until they were adults.

At times, our father would drive us along the West Side Highway near the piers to show us the ocean liners. Each of us had our own designated ship. Angie's was the *Queen Elizabeth* and mine was the *Queen Mary*. From the car, we would gaze at these monstrous ships and imagine the faraway places that they were going to.

These trips also allowed us to see how other people lived. For example, our father would show us the Hotel Carlisle where President Kennedy would stay when in New York, and he would speak to us about the various important monuments, such as Grant's tomb, while en route to our destination. One night, he took us to Harlem to the Theresa Hotel where Fidel Castro was staying. The crowds were huge and the police presence was intense. At times, we would drive down Fifth Avenue and wave at the doormen, confused and bewildered about the need to have someone open your door.

In contrast, while visiting our grandmother in Harlem or some of our distant cousins throughout different ghettos in New York City, we realized that some people lived in even more impoverished conditions than we did. At a very young age, we became aware that the world was a far larger place than Patterson Projects or whatever neighborhood we were living in at the time and that this world was composed of many different persons, events, and things.

These trips were extremely rare, but perhaps their infrequency contributed to their profound impact on us. One visit to the Museum of Hispanic Art and another to the Metropolitan Museum of Art, for example, left us with permanent images of huge paintings and with an actual personal experience of how art can make a difference in one's life.

Social gatherings would often turn into lengthy dialogues with friends and family about world politics and other subjects. Our father's interests in politics, literature, history, and art, as well as his daily attention to newspapers, radio, and TV news, were also factors that contributed to our viewing ourselves as part of something that was larger than our immediate surroundings. His comments about the Yankee propaganda in the media and his long discourses about the ills of imperialism, capitalism, and colonialism left us with an understanding that the news was something to respond to rather than merely accept.

Walter Cronkite, David Brinkley, and Chet Huntley, the major news anchors on television, were people not to be trusted. However, what they said was important enough to listen to. Moreover, our father's activism in the Puerto Rican Independence Movement served to instill in us a sense of idealism, a respect for the workingman, a concern for the poor, a sense of responsibility for the underdog, and an understanding of the role of class and race in this society.

Our father's immense love for poetry and his outstanding skill in its delivery provided us with an appreciation of the written word as well as of performance. His love for the arts was so great that at a time in our lives when we were at our poorest—our high school years—my father surprised us with tickets to the Bolshoi Ballet at Carnegie Hall. This might account for the fact that we were always at least one month behind in the rent and lacked the money for such items as clothes and dental services, which my father viewed as unimportant. However, it also accounts for our having a world that was larger than that of our friends, who could only imagine some of the things that we had actually experienced.

Our father's living for the moment philosophy was very different from my mother's middle-class perspective. Nonetheless, both respected each other's interests and more importantly, both shared a common bond—namely, a respect and value for knowledge. From a very early age, we knew that there was a reason for school and this reason was connected to our future.

Our mother's familial background was instrumental in molding her views on education, which centered on the practical reasons for an education. My father, on the other hand, focused more on ideological and experiential concerns. Nonetheless, their great respect for education had an impact on our attitudes about school.

The fact that our maternal grandfather was a judge in Puerto Rico and was educated in Spain and that several of my mother's siblings were college graduates facilitated our knowing about the positive impact school could have on your life. In my mother's case, this was particularly true. Here she found herself, a daughter of a professional, who as a young girl had experienced a privileged life, living in conditions that were unimaginable to most of her family members. We witnessed firsthand the power of choices and the power of not having an education and knowing the language, as was the case of our father. We repeatedly witnessed that being schooled and being educated are two distinct things. Our father was an extremely educated man without the adequate schooling.

Our mother's reverence for her family, despite our not even knowing these relatives who lived on the island, was so profound that we often felt that we could not replicate their achievements. At times, this reverence worked to undermine our abilities, but in another way it provided us with a value, and even more importantly, a reason for going to school.

Knowledge regarding the purpose of school and the meaningful connection with a child's life is, not surprisingly, a factor that can impact on school engagement and his or her academic aspirations (Kincheloe & Steinberg, 2000). Absence of such knowledge, leading to a discontinuity between school and home, can have a detrimental impact on a child's academic performance. Unfortunately, the poor, who frequently experience this lack of connection, opt to leave school. Instead of finding ways to engage such students, rationalizations in order to justify such school abandonment are made regarding their inability to delay gratification or their values. The poor are viewed as a population without self-control who, because of such weakness, find themselves in unfavorable circumstances. This need to engage in immediate gratification, an animal-like attribute, is often ascribed to them rather than to the failure of schools to connect with children. As cited in Hale (2001, p. 175), children who cannot conceptualize a future for themselves do not have the motivation to defer the gratification found in premature sexual activity or substance abuse. Such views about children of color fail to understand that oftentimes school achievement is more about having a purpose or reason to engage in a process that can possibly be boring, dehumanizing, and painful rather than about lacking the ability to delay pleasure.

Chapter Ten

Curriculum

The reformulation of the United States from a melting pot into a pluralistic society has been a relatively new phenomenon of the past two decades. The Puerto Rican population of the 1950s and 1960s was caught in the transition period—a collision between ideology and reality. The period was a time of contradictions, confusion, and pain when viewed through the lens of the Puerto Rican reality, which centered on segregation in tenements situated in ethnic enclaves in selected areas of New York City and employment in menial jobs with little room for social mobility. We were told that all immigrants came to this nation and were absorbed into the melting pot and thus were led to believe that our future would soon follow this same path. However, our reality did not reflect such an experience, leading to false assumptions about why we could not "make it," assumptions centered on notions of inability, laziness, refusal, and many more explanations used to rationalize why our patterns of assimilation did not follow prior white European immigrations.

Schools did not provide clarity in understanding our situation. Schools remained true to a traditional Eurocentric view of knowledge that served to promote Western Civilization and disregard the rest of the planet's population. What we learned is what fit into the paradigm of Western Civilization being superior to all other cultures. This experience is referred to by Lewis (1996, p.36) as the

> double-cross-reversal: the privilege of the dominant to talk at great length about that which is not and to stay silent about and ignore that which is. In this reversal, for socially subordinate groups, possibility is defined through denial, freedom is reinterpreted through constraint, violence is justified as protection, and in schools, contrary to the belief that

it is a place where knowledge is shared, knowledge withheld articulates the curriculum.

Throughout our education little was taught about Puerto Rico or its people. The one thing that we did learn was that Puerto Rico was given to the United States after the Spanish-American War. The island was also used as an example of a Third World nation and an example of a poor country with uneducated people who were being saved from greater poverty by the United States. Furthermore, the United States opened its doors to us and provided us with the opportunity to improve our lives. Imagine, we had the opportunity to become civilized and maybe if we played our cards right we would move out of the ghetto.

What these teachers did not tell us was that after the Spanish-American War, Puerto Rico was given to the United States without the consent of its people. Puerto Rico went from having a fairly autonomous relationship with Spain to one of colonial dependency with the United States. They also failed to inform us that American corporations had taken over Puerto Rican agriculture and transformed it from a self-sufficient multicrop economy into a mono-crop sugar economy, which later resulted in adverse economic conditions that subsequently resulted in our migration to the United States. Furthermore, many of my friends' fathers, including mine, were drafted and had fought in World War II. In fact, the 65th infantry division was from Puerto Rico, a fact I did not know until I was an adolescent. Also, these very same soldiers who had been on the front did not have the right to vote in federal elections while in Puerto Rico, a right that many did not exercise until they came and settled in New York after having defended America.

More importantly, what they did not tell us was that our migration to New York City in the 1950s during a period when industries were leaving the city for more profitable localities would become for many Puerto Ricans a road to low-paying menial jobs for several generations to come. The timing of our move to New York City was unfortunate. Here we were in segregated ghettos in a city that did not have the economic opportunities that previous immigrants had profited from. Our lack of economic prosperity and social mobility was thought to be due to our lack of desire to progress rather than as the by-product of a postindustrial economy that did not meet the needs of a population that came to work in industries that were leaving New York.

As Pinar (1996, p. 23) explains:

> We are what we know and also what we do not know. If what we know about ourselves—history, our culture, our national identity—is deformed by absences, denials and incompleteness, then our identity—both as individuals and as Americans—is fractured.

Such omissions regarding our place in history and our relationship to the United States are crucial. They transformed issues of colonialism, American economics, and military interests into personalized concerns of indebtedness for America's generosity without an understanding of why and how we ended up on the mainland. If curriculum is supposed to facilitate our understanding of the world (Grumet, 1996), then one can say that our curriculum provided us with an inaccurate purview.

What this does to a child's psyche is destructive. It tells you that you are poor and this host nation is doing you a favor by allowing you to be here. This one-sided view results in you blaming yourself and in particular your parents for your unfortunate place in American society. This facilitates the internalization of negative beliefs and stereotypes about one's culture and the inevitable acceptance of such beliefs by all, including yourself.

You are like an uninvited guest at a formal dinner party that is reserved for those of a particular group, namely, white and European. You are hastily seated at the table but find yourself without eating utensils. The devastating effect that this situation has on a child who is forming his/her self-image and starting to make judgments about what he/she is capable or incapable of cannot be understated.

Chapter Eleven

Motivation

School Achievement

We found ourselves asking some questions over and over during the course of writing our childhood experiences, such as: What kept us engaged in school, and why did some of our friends faced with similar situations decide to drop out of school or opt not to pursue a higher education? With regard to those who did complete high school, most of them did not strive for academic excellence. They were quite content to attain whatever was necessary to merely obtain a high school diploma. At a time when not everyone was expected to go to college and less so for a Puerto Rican female in the Bronx, the decision to get married and/or go to work would have been perfectly acceptable courses for our lives.

Alma

Nonetheless, both of us decided to go to college and ultimately complete doctorate degrees, rejecting the most logical and accessible courses. Why? This question has been posed to us on many occasions. Both of us have always succeeded in academia. Throughout her schooling, Angie was repeatedly the top performer in school, regardless of level, type of school, the school's racial and ethnic composition, grade, or subject. As for me, the less conscientious student of the two of us, I have always been a high performer. We have repeatedly excelled in the classroom, despite adverse situations at home and school.

In search of a theoretical explanation for the sources of our engagement in school, we examined the psychological literature on school achievement. The search yielded few clear answers. One reason is that the literature itself does not employ a global perspective. It addresses aspects of a person's behavior without examining it in a social context where class, race, ethnicity, and teacher competency, to name just a few variables, intersect and impact on a person's academic performance (Villanueva, 1993). Nonetheless, this exercise did yield insights into what things were valid for us and what factors, although proven to impact on school achievement, did not play a significant role in our lives. In fact, many of the behaviors, attitudes, and learning environments that the research indicates promote school engagement were undoubtedly the opposite or nonexistent in our school experience, causing even more questions to emerge.

The implications of our findings lead us to conclude that one must be very careful about making assumptions regarding student achievement. The use of labels to categorize pupils according to attribution style, kinds of motivation, or goal orientation could prove to be useless and at times detrimental. We found that motivation for both of us has been a fluid factor in our lives. It has fluctuated according to our situation at the time, and it is better understood in a continuum that flows from sources of school achievement due to fear of punishment to the highest form of internal motivation—the pure pleasure that one attains while engaging in learning.

The majority of research findings ultimately define motivation as the force that directs, energizes, and sustains behavior. It is what makes us go in a particular direction and keeps us going. The research is vast, with early behavioral studies examining reinforcement as the source of human behavior. Subsequent studies, known as social learning theories, focus on the role that modeling and observation play in learning and development.

Additional studies look at traits and focus on such motives as a need for affiliation, a need for approval, and a need for achievement, while other research addresses the social dynamics of peer groups. Lastly, some inquiries examine the cognitive perspectives of motivation. This latter category represents the current view regarding motivation. These studies now consider human motivation as a function of human cognition involving inquisitiveness, goal setting, and development of interest in particular areas. Research in this area addresses student behavior and the characteristics of learning environments in promoting engagement in school.

Students with High Achievement Motivation

In general, what these more recent studies tell us is that intrinsic motivation plays an important role in promoting school engagement. In this case, intrinsic motivation is viewed as behavior that is performed out of internal interest and requires no external prods, promises, or threats. Its emergence stems from our sense of self and is self-determined. At the highest level of intrinsic motivation, there is no awareness of means-end separation. There is no goal separate from the ongoing activity (Brophy, 1998).

Deci and Ryan (1991) view intrinsic motivation in terms of the presence of subjective perceptions of self-determination rather than in terms of the absence of extrinsic incentives. This definition acknowledges the possible existence of extrinsic motivators at the same time that one is self-motivated.

High achievers are often less focused on receiving external rewards for learning. They derive pleasure from mastering tasks and exhibit a willingness to take risks and make mistakes; they focus on making sense of subject matter rather than on rote memorization of facts; and they initiate learning activities in a particular domain. These students exhibit eagerness to explore and learn.

Successful students also are characterized as having mastery goals exemplified by a desire to acquire additional knowledge or master new skills. This differs from someone identified as having performance goals that entail completing a task to look good or receive favorable judgments from others.

Additional findings inform us that successful students perceive their successes and failures in given ways. When asked about their future, they anticipate that they will continue to succeed, while children who don't achieve in school predict that they will always fail.

Moreover, the most optimistic students are those who attribute their successes to such things as innate ability and their failures to lack of effort or the use of inappropriate strategies. Students who achieve in school more often attribute their success and failures to their actions than those who do not succeed. Less successful students view success or failure as being something external over which they have no control. For example, they would most likely attribute success in school to luck, and failure to the teacher not liking them.

This kind of attribution leads to self-defeating thoughts such as the following: If success and failure are external and not possible to control, then why even attempt to succeed? This results in disengagement in school.

Studies that focus on student interaction inform us about the importance of friends, cliques, and crowds in high school and the significance of these groups in determining an adolescent's academic performance. Those students who identify and value high performers will identify with that larger group, while others who opt for popularity will sacrifice academic performance for social acceptance.

Learning Environments

To foster engagement in the classroom, educators are urged to promote intrinsic motivation by focusing students' attention away from external consequences and emphasizing internal pleasures such as feelings of pride, satisfaction, and the employment that academic tasks can yield. According to Deci and Ryan (1994), self-determination is promoted in classrooms that provide students with meaningful rationales that will aid them in comprehending the purpose and personal importance of each learning activity. Such classrooms also acknowledge students' sentiments regarding unfavorable tasks that they might be asked to do and provide students with choices rather than control.

Furthermore, educators are warned against the overuse of external reinforcements such as grades, free time, or special privileges. If external reinforcements are used, teachers should use praise to communicate information and enhance students' self-efficacy and sense of competency. It is also recommended that students be exposed to successful models who are similar to them.

In addition, competition and comparisons should be minimized; the focus should be on the individual improvement of the student. Teachers should emphasize mastery goals over performance goals by focusing on the process that students used rather than on the final outcome.

Students should be given encouraging messages regarding the causes of their successes and failures. It is also suggested that teachers have students realize that some successes come only with considerable effort and perseverance. Although the need for rules and procedures in the classroom is acknowledged, the teacher should employ them without communicating a message of extreme control. Such a strategy will set the tone of the class toward a path of maintaining students' sense of self-determination. Lastly, it is recommended that teachers tailor their motivational strategies toward the needs and motives of individual students. They should use different reinforcements to meet the needs of different students and be attentive to the needs of students at risk or those with a high probability of failing to acquire the minimum academic skills necessary.

Our Perspectives on Our Motives for Learning

In reviewing our attitudes about school engagement and achievement, we found that, although we were siblings and had attended the same or similar schools, our individual views were very different.

Angie revealed that she had always enjoyed learning. When hospitalized at a very young age, she remembers a teacher provided by social services had brought a workbook to her bedside and told her to complete a few pages. When the teacher returned she was amazed to see that Angie had completed the entire book. She was enjoying herself so much that she did not consider what the teacher gave her to be an assignment. Regardless of what she was doing, whether it was coloring in a coloring book, working on a puzzle, or reading a book, Angie remembers enjoying being totally submerged in the particular activity. Her enjoyment came from doing the best she could and completing the particular task. During play, she would pretend to be in school and often took the role of the teacher. Moreover, she never really disliked any subject area.

In school she had all As. If a class was somewhat boring, it became a challenge for her to master the material. She would find the beauty of the discipline. It was very difficult for her to decide on a major, because she found most subjects captivating. What would possibly start as a dull assignment for a term paper would end up being an intriguing bit of knowledge that she treasured. Once she put her energy into something, she became enthralled with it.

She changed her major nine times in college because she could not decide which subject she preferred. After successfully completing the coursework for a premed program, she decided to major in psychology. This, however, came after a significant accumulation of credits in other areas.

But her primary reason for going to college was her commitment to learning and to furthering her education. The assignment in her first essay in freshman English Composition was to write about her career goals. She wrote about wanting to be an "educated bum." Despite her talents, she did not approach school with any future practical concerns. However, school also represented her only means of improving her life.

In spite of all the reasons centered around her love of learning, Angie also admits that her engagement in school as a young girl was also due to her fear of the nuns' punitive ways. For her, school was a way out of the ghetto.

Angie

Alma, on the other hand, remembers deriving great pleasure from bicycle riding and jumping Double Dutch and engaging in particular school tasks, but these occurrences were few and far between. She does not recall getting a great deal of pleasure from school. Becoming educated for her was not an unbearable burden. It was a doable task that demanded a reasonable amount of time and effort.

She did enjoy history and math, but had almost no interest at all in other subjects. However, she did not hate any particular area of study. Her main reasons for engaging in school were threefold. First, with a sister like me, who was such a high achiever, she felt obligated to perform for fear of being considered stupid. Second, as a young child she feared the nuns; and third, as she got older, she realized that those who went on to higher education were usually the white kids. These were the kids who usually did not live in the neighborhood. They lived in private homes, had Sweet Sixteen parties, and wore nice clothes. They must be doing something right, she thought.

Although as an adolescent a way out of poverty was her primary reason for school engagement, as she advanced in high school she took pleasure in being recognized for her academic performance. Her Latino friends, who were not tremendously high achievers, recognized her accomplishments. They referred to her as "the brain." She began to sense that she was unusual among her clique, and that this uniqueness was a good thing. She found that her friends valued her success. It was not until her activism in college and her engagement in ethnic studies that she began to truly enjoy learning without necessarily having a goal in mind.

Alma feels that had she not been my sister, she most likely would have been an average student who probably would have been married at a very young age and never gone on to college. Most likely, she would have been a secretary or a hairdresser, the two careers that her mother had selected for her. Alma attributes her mother's aspirations for her to the roles of women at that time and to the comparison of my outstanding academic performance to her very good but inferior performance.

Being a mother and a homemaker was the course taken by many of her friends. She recalls being a bridesmaid or maid of honor in at least five weddings within the year following her high school graduation. Even many of her friends who were on an academic track did not go on to higher education, and those who did decided not to continue. Alma's lack of interest in getting married and her focus on school became a source of interest for her friends. At one wedding, the bride purposely threw the bouquet of flowers directly at her.

Even though both of us were very good students, we both expressed a lack of confidence in attaining our goals. I had been accepted into several Ivy League colleges and been provided with scholarships, but still had a deep recurring feeling that I wasn't smart enough. Alma had similar feelings about succeeding in college, but these sentiments were compounded by doubts of whether or not she had the tenacity to hang in there because her love for school was not great. Furthermore, we both firmly believed that school would greatly influence our future lives.

Alma

Angie, who derived pleasure from the mere act of learning, seems to have always been intrinsically motivated. Her feelings existed prior to the emergence of her awareness concerning the material benefits that can be derived from a good education. Angie enjoyed learning, and because she was successful at it, doing well in school became a way of feeling good about herself and getting recognition.

Angie also admits to being motivated to achieve because she wanted to prove to her white classmates that she was their equal. This is not unusual for students of color, who at times exhibit a need to overachieve in order to disprove negative assumptions made about their racial or ethnic group (Donaldson, 1994; Spencer, 2001). Unfortunately, because she always excelled academically, she felt that she was expected to always do well, and in the latter part of high school, this expectation became a burden that interfered with the fun of learning.

The process of applying to colleges in her senior year was gruesome. There was an inordinate amount of pressure to perform and get into the right school. Previously, Angela had been satisfied with the thought of attending City College. Now, she found herself on the track to go to Harvard. She felt that she had to compete and accomplish. The intrinsic goal of learning was now confounded with pleasing her father, her teachers, and her guidance counselor. At one point, she felt that she was doing it for the entire island of Puerto Rico.

Angie

On the other hand, Alma saw success in school as a means of doing what she thought was expected of her and saving face. It was a way to escape negative consequences, as well as a means to an end. In high school, when fear of the nuns' wrath was absent, Alma began to value her academic success and saw it as a necessary factor for admission into college. In essence, her extrinsic motivation was transformed from being grounded in fear and the opinions of others to something that was personally valued and integrated into her everyday life. It was not until the latter part of her college career, when she began to learn about her culture and history and became involved in the political movement of the '60s, that she began to derive pleasure from learning, and the source of her behavior became an intrinsic force. Like Alma, I viewed education as a way out of my present situation. My love of learning from a very young age and the energy I put into the quality of my work were more important to me than getting a diploma. When I think of school, I think of the pleasure that stemmed from my engagement in the academic process.

When we talked about success and failure, we each took responsibility for how we did in school. During her junior year in high school, for example, Alma was working from 2:00 to 8:00 p.m. at Dr. Levine's, a dental clinic on 138th Street in the South Bronx, and she was also placed in all honor classes. In addition, she fell head over heels for a guy who attended Cardinal Hayes High School, resulting in the plummeting of her grades during the last marking period of her junior year. While she was still able to graduate in the top five percent of her class, she attributes the lousy grades in physics and trigonometry to her own lack of effort.

Alma

Angie's own lack of confidence, despite an overall average of 95, resulted in her studying night and day. I remember how our room was covered from floor to ceiling with formulas that Angie was learning. It was not unusual for her to wake up in the middle of the night and put on the light and review her notes. I also remember Angie taking long subway rides so she could study for her regents. I would study on the fire escape in order to get away from the noise coming from my father's music, but riding back and forth on the number six subway line was a little too extreme for me. Frankly, I found my sister's behavior to be bizarre. Although extreme, Angie, too, took responsibility for the outcome of her grades. Neither of us ever felt that our grades were due to anything except our individual efforts, and less importantly, our abilities.

One variable that could have contributed to our academic achievement in high school in particular was our friends. The literature states that the intimate group, the clique, and the crowd are instrumental in determining academic achievement (Steinberg, 1998). The intimate group consists of a few close friends; the clique is a larger group with which one either socializes, eats lunch, or participates in various activities. Lastly, the crowd is a construct, which refers to how one sees oneself within the entire school. Not surprisingly, Angie's friends, clique, and crowd consisted of high achievers. Although her very close friends were not as high achieving as she was, they were all college bound and, with the exception of one, members of the Honor School.

Angie

As usual, Alma's situation was different from mine. Most of her inner circle of friends consisted of students who were not part of the Honor School. Some had no intention of going to college, while others, despite their mediocre performance, intended to pursue higher education. Nonetheless, as part of the Honor School she saw herself as a high achiever within the larger crowd.

The examination of our motives, school associations, and attributions of success and failures related to our school performance yielded interesting results. While it became clear that my intrinsic source of motivation was a significant force for my accomplishments, after reviewing the literature, we found that Alma's pattern of behavior was more the norm. It is not uncommon for children to exhibit intrinsic motivation very early in their educational career with an increase in extrinsic motivation and hopefully back to intrinsic in the higher grades. In Alma's case, college was the pivotal arena.

Alma

Angie's continued motivation was unusual, however. Such a stable and consistent degree of intrinsic motivation could be what distinguishes an average or good student from an outstanding one. What our findings did not yield were answers to why, if my pattern of behavior was not unusual, did the rest of my Latino friends not succeed in the same way? This led us to look at the one variable that did distinguish me from the rest, namely, my big sister Angie, who represented a model for me. This is consistent with social learning theory that refers to models of behavior and the importance of these models in impacting on the behavior of others. This also provides credence to the role of the older sibling in setting the standard for those who follow.

Our look at the social dynamics in and out of school found that while we had distinct kinds of friends, there was one common factor that our friends placed value on, academic success, even in cases where some were at the lower end of the school performance scale. The value placed on our achievement by our peers enhanced our status within our groups. It also gave us permission to aspire within the larger crowd, as was my case. I had many friends who were underachievers, but they did not view me as a social misfit or as being "white," a dichotomy that is often detrimental to the academic achievement of African American males (Ogbu, 1994). One explanation could be that we were all first-generation Puerto Ricans or newly migrated Puerto Ricans or Cubans. As documented in the literature, we had not yet taken on the assimilated values found in many current educational institutions, where academic achievement is not valued over being popular or being a jock (Steinberg, 1998).

It might have also been a sign of the times when academic achievement was something to emulate and not scorn.

Our Perspectives on Our Learning Environments

Angie

The area found to have the greatest discrepancy between our lives was in the classroom. We both concluded that our school experiences, in particular our elementary years completed in Catholic schools, were characterized by an atmosphere of corporal punishment, high degrees of focus on grades, and fierce competition instead of learning for the sake of development. Teaching was grounded in behavioral approaches based on extrinsic reinforcements, which were usually punishments. Our weekly activities centered on spelling bees, pop quizzes, and a multitude of tests. Classrooms were decorated with tests of students who scored 100% and bulletin boards that reflected how many stars we had accumulated for good behavior. One's accumulation of stars could yield favorable or unfavorable results depending on what end of the scale that your stars fell.

Furthermore, students were rarely given choices or opportunities to explore anything beyond what was given to them. A low grade was never seen as an opportunity to learn from one's mistakes. Failure meant one thing, more work, and possibly punish lessons. Even when engaging in an enjoyable task such as writing about a personal interest, one would be careful to write in short, nonflowery language for fear that a comma, period, or modifier would be incorrectly placed. Such a violation of correct grammatical usage would automatically result in a failing grade, and an additional assignment would be required. Erasures on math tests written with fountain pens would automatically give you a zero.

Teachers repeatedly used the same methods to give instruction, which did little to stimulate students or address the needs of those who might have their understanding enhanced through a different approach. Lesson plans did not consider learning styles, communicative approaches, zones of proximal development, or learning deficiency. The target was the average student, who was taught through rote memorization, seated work, and repetitious activities with a teacher-centered approach in an overcrowded classroom and with far too many students for such a small room. The "pedagogy of poverty" was the norm rather than the exception (Haberman, 1991).

Although our high school experience was far from the ideal learning environment for us, it was an improvement from our experiences in grammar school. As members of the Honor School, we had the best teachers. Unfortunately, the rest of the population, which consisted predominantly of students of color, was not privy to this level of instruction. If on occasion, for programmatic reasons, one was placed in a nonhonors class, as Alma was in one or two classes, the difference in pedagogy, curriculum, and student engagement would be witnessed.

While the external sources of reinforcement, such as grades and the ultimate goal of a diploma, were still present, the great difference for us between high school and grammar school was the absence of castigation for not knowing, doing, or understanding. Failure in school would now translate into personal disappointment and responsibility rather than fear.

Our recollections of many of our high school teachers are of educators who came to class prepared to teach, encourage student participation, and inspire us to learn. Both of us recall looking forward to having certain teachers because of their mastery in teaching.

Alma

In high school, competition also took on a different form. The grammar school practice of having stars, stickers, and papers hung up on bulletin boards was replaced by the tracking of students. Our segregation as members of the Honor School in itself set up a competitive situation, but each of us had a different experience. Angie's number one status, which on occasion fluctuated to number two, was characterized by more pressure to maintain her heavyweight crown.

My response to my sister's exceptional accomplishments was not to compete. At a very early age I realized that trying to attain Angie's level of achievement was not something that I wished to strive for, and quite frankly, it was something that I knew I might not be able to accomplish. Nonetheless, while we did not compete with each other, there were teachers who were constantly comparing us, and in this case, I was at a disadvantage.

A competitive climate was also sustained by the tracking of students in academic, secretarial, and general programs. Students in academic programs were those expecting to go to college, while those on a secretarial track were usually females who were being prepared to be secretaries. Lastly, those in general programs seemed to be the students without many goals. The least numbers of African American and Latino students were found in the academic track—a fact documented in the literature (Oakes, 1992). At a time when the Vietnam War was at its peak and the City University of New York required the completion of certain academic subjects as entrance requirements, students in the general track, unless blessed with a high draft lottery number, were faced with being drafted shortly after high school. Not surprisingly, these were the racial minorities, many of who were members of my circle of friends.

While reflecting on the reasons that engaged us in school, both Angie and I agreed that teacher expectations played a major role in motivating us. In Catholic school, students were expected to perform regardless of differences in race, background, or ability. Although the absence of attention placed on differences in ability or student preparedness did impact negatively on students who needed such attention, it sent a clear message to the rest of the student body, namely, that you could and were expected to learn. Student engagement, although driven by fear, was expected and required of all.

While the methods employed by many of our teachers did not foster the most challenging and stimulating environments, as proposed by Escalante in Meek (1989), they were to some extent effective. Students studied and learned, but often for the wrong reasons and at the expense of critical thought. While the atmosphere in which we received our education was a far cry from an ideal learning environment, in retrospect it was still better than what many of our children now experience, which is an almost total absence of teaching or learning, because they are in the hands of professionals who very often possess preconceived notions about who they are and what they can do. While the unorthodox approaches used by some of our teachers resulted in many students not wishing to continue in higher education—despite the economic advantages, social status, and other benefits of having a degree—they did send a message that students were expected to learn, and could learn.

Our segregation in the Honor School and the privileges that came with such membership were also important factors in our success in school. In this case, teachers' expectations, as well as the expectations of our fellow classmates, served as a source of motivation.

Summary

Explanations of our academic achievement that centered on issues of motivation and effective pedagogy were found to give inadequate understanding as to why both of us made the choices that we did. For years, we were led to believe by teachers and neighbors that we were exceptions, and for this reason we achieved the way that we did. These assumptions about us caused much conflict, pain, and confusion throughout our development. The mixed messages of inferiority, superiority, worthiness, and unworthiness were embedded into our lives on a daily basis in one way or another. Yes, we were exceptions, but not because of an innate superiority or an accident of nature that distinguished us from our fellow Nuyoricans; it was because of a unique combination of factors and fate and our responses to these forces. This aggregation of variables is what makes traditional notions of school success inadequate in explaining our school performance or, for that matter, the academic performance of those who do not fall within the norm.

Our home, while poor, unstable, and dysfunctional, did provide us with a sense of the importance of education for both ideological and instrumental reasons. Early knowledge of the role of school and its importance in our future lives was something that was taught to us at home. The desire to learn and knowledge about an education system and how to negotiate such a system were the greatest gifts that our parents bestowed on us.

Furthermore, our childhood in the projects provided us with a sense of belonging, acceptance, and community that formed our early ideas about people and about ourselves in particular. The insulation of the projects and our engagement in the lives of our neighbors, as well as their roles in our lives, created for us an environment that permitted us to grow in the absence of an abundance of detrimental and stereotypical views of race, ethnicity, and class. Although television disregarded our existence and at times contributed to the fueling of negative images about blacks and Latinos in particular, our daily experiences did not reinforce these images. The importance of these ethnic cocoons in molding our early self-concepts must be recognized.

Our early experiences with our beloved and not-so-beloved nuns in Catholic school, while instilling in us terror rather than a desire to learn, did provide us with enough fear to propel us to engage in learning for a significant segment of our childhood. While this trepidation, for many students, served as a future detriment to their continuing school, our early successes in this domain served as external sources of motivation to become engaged learners. The success of Catholic schools in teaching children of color, as cited in Nite (1996 p. 244) has been documented.

The nuns' uniformity of expectations for all, although detrimental to those students who could not succeed or for the students who warranted a difference in approaches, enabled those who could to excel. Fortunately, we were in the group of successful students. For those who fell behind and could not meet such expectations, school became a continuous nightmare of intimidation and a source of pain and fear.

When we left the projects and attended a more racially and ethnically segregated school, the negative messages we internalized began to tear away at the strong self-concept that we had formed while in our ethnic enclave. This propelled Angie to become extremely achievement oriented in order to dispel those negative messages about Puerto Ricans. I became as disengaged as I could without sacrificing academic performance.

In high school, our membership in a predominantly white Honor School exposed us to a quality and consistency of teaching not always accessible to those students who were not part of this privileged group. We also escaped the possibility of being tracked into dead-end vocational or commercial programs. Those outside the Honor School were usually students of color. While this presented problems of loneliness, not being part of the Honor School cliques never forced us to have to choose between who we were as students and our ethnicity or race. In my case, I never had to make a choice between being an honor student and my peer group—a choice forced on many minority youths (Mahiri, 1998). The support and acceptance that I found with my Latino friends, who were often not on an academic track and were lower academic achievers, were invaluable advantages during adolescence when such acceptance is crucial. The recognition by these friends of my academic achievement and the niche that I made for myself within this group were instrumental in the choices that I made.

Angie was also fortunate to be a member of a group of four students, all black or Latino, who were some of the few persons of color in the Honor School who shared similar goals and aspirations. This, particularly for Angie, who was at the top of her class, became a refuge from an environment that was often competitive and alienating.

Our experiences in Puerto Rico, although intensely traumatic, forced us to make crucial decisions regarding who we were racially and ethnically. Most important was that we chose who we were rather than let traditional and arbitrary designations of race and ethnicity be thrust upon us. This strength and pride in who we were was crucial at a time in American history when such a designation was often detrimental. We were in fact Nuyoricans or Puerto Ricans from New York who were persons of color. For us, as well as for many other such persons during this time, this was not an easy choice in a society that recognized only black or white. Like many others, we were two sisters who could have easily passed for white, but in the process of making such a choice, we would have also forfeited our souls and spirits.

The strength we derived from this stance fueled our future choices, which also led to unlikely courses of action for two such siblings at that point in time.

Chapter Twelve

Multicultural Education

The story of our childhood educational experiences is not much different from that of other first-generation American-born children prior to the latter part of the twentieth century. We were educated in an environment that stressed the importance of homogeneity and one that was unforgiving to those who could not put aside their uniqueness. Differences among us were not measured by who was educated or how we were educated but in the outcome of that process. Many of those immigrant children, first-generation Puerto Rican children in particular, failed to complete school, as reflected in the prison population, welfare rolls, and poverty levels.

Nonetheless, many did graduate from high school and were absorbed by New York City's economy. This was possible because such a market had room for entry-level jobs found in the garment industry and other areas of manufacturing. However, the city's manufacturing-based economy would soon be transformed into one driven by information and banking. The ocean of garment trucks; factories with rows of sewing machines, each attended by a seamstress; and smokestacks with smells of chemicals emerging from various plants scattered throughout the city would give way to neatly manicured offices, each boasting the latest technology. More importantly, the dingy warehouses and factories, often populated by persons with not much education and a limited knowledge of English, were now replaced by office buildings full of college graduates with strong literacy skills and higher-order thinking skills. There was now very little room for those who did not have the skills to compete in such an environment.

One cannot help but wonder what happened to the many people we knew who at one time were part of this blue-collar working force. They were part of the mass that pushed the clothing carts in the garment industry, sewed the clothes, packed the garments in the shipping departments, swept the floors, and stood on assembly lines. These were the laborers who very often worked forty-plus hours a week in conditions that were not the best but who at the end of the week could gain some satisfaction from knowing that they were contributing, however meagerly, to the support of their families.

These were our former schoolmates, whom we would recognize and greet in the subway on our way to college and on their way to work. For those who did not work in the factory, a clerical position or one in the mailroom was a step up from their parents' daily toil. While some made the transition necessary to meet the needs of the "new" New York, others joined the welfare rolls, unemployment lines, and prison population. For those who followed this generation and found themselves smack in the middle of an information-driven economy without any work experience and with an absence of skills to meet the demands of a technological society, the future was even more dismal.

In essence, many of the Nuyoricans attending school during the 1950s and 1960s were educated to meet the demands of those decades but found themselves in a pivotal period unprepared to meet the demands of the city's new economic order. They were the products of an education system that only knew how to function by proceeding forward regardless of the disparity in success and failures as measured by race, ethnicity, or socioeconomic group. This was a system that ignored the diversity of the population that it was teaching. Only when these failures were of such a magnitude that they could not be ignored did school officials begin to rethink their approach. Now, poor academic achievement was not confined to the African American, Puerto Rican, and poor white populations but also included a growing number of Dominicans, West Indians, Colombians, and many more who, because of the change in the immigration laws, began to grow in numbers. Thus, the population of persons of color, who at one time had been a relatively small group, now became the population of the Big Apple, and the need for major systemic changes became obvious. Not until this school-age population became significant in numbers and failure rates continued to rise were questions about how and why asked and addressed. While the questions continue to be asked, solutions to such issues are few.

One possible remedy that has emerged as a response to the challenge of educating a diverse population is that of a multicultural approach to education. This method addresses many of the concerns about how we were taught that surfaced while writing this book. While we both survived and succeeded as a consequence of our education, many whom we knew did not. We were the exception, as reflected in the low high school completion rates and low representation of Hispanics in higher education. The dismal numbers of our generation who completed high school, and the even smaller numbers who continued their education, provide testimony to the idea that the ways that children are taught must validate who they are in order to be effective. This is particularly true for children who come from homes where the culture is greatly different from that of the classroom. In addition, children do not all learn in the same way.

Nieto (1996, p. 308–323), when speaking of multicultural education, describes an approach that is antiracist. Such an approach is attentive to all areas in which some students may be favored over others. These areas include the curriculum, choice of materials, sorting policies, and teachers' interactions and relationships with students and their communities. Nieto proposes that multicultural education must be related to the core curriculum. It should permeate every aspect of school, including the school climate, physical environment, and curriculum as well as the relationships among teacher and students and community. It must be included as a basic part of the curriculum rather than as a peripheral activity or interest. Not surprisingly, the canon must be transformed and expanded to include those cultures and people who have been traditionally excluded. The expansive nature of multicultural education makes it a process for all rather than something that is only for students of color, urban students, or the disadvantaged. Lastly, multicultural education is a process that is ongoing and dynamic, with the purpose of putting our learning into action. In essence, education should be socially beneficial and meaningful. Schools should be sites of apprenticeship for democracy. If the aforementioned model of multicultural education had been the norm during our education, we would have had very different educational experiences. The expansion of the canon to include other cultures would in itself have made all of us better educated individuals. Yes, even that white Irish Catholic friend of Angie's, whose mother would not permit us into her home because we were Puerto Rican, might now have understood that our presence in New York was due to the same kind of economic reasons as those of her family. Maybe this knowledge would not have gotten us through the door, but hopefully her mother's prejudice would have been questioned rather than internalized by a child who did not know better.

In essence, the benefits of a multicultural curriculum are not only in how it helps children of nonmainstream cultures, but also in how it educates children of the majority culture. Everyone's ignorance of non-European cultures, histories, and religions when completing secondary school would have most likely been replaced by a better understanding and appreciation of Native American, African, Asian, and Latin American cultures. More importantly, the inclusion of where we came from, the contributions of our ancestors, and the forces that impacted on our parents' migration to the United States would have given us a better perspective about who we were.

The effect of such knowledge on the lives of young children and adolescents must be underscored. Those feelings of anomie, incompetence, inferiority, and shame that we experienced very often, despite our outward attainment of success, would have been nonexistent and possibly replaced by feelings that would have facilitated success and social participation. Possibly, our choices would have been different, or at least clarity about our paths would have emerged earlier. Even more so, the emotional, psychological, and spiritual price we paid for success would have been less. For children who did not succeed and paid a greater price by living in poverty for the rest of their lives, and having a string of dead-end jobs that day in and day out reminded them of the need for an education without any hope of one, such an approach to education as proposed by Nieto would have certainly had an impact on their lives.

Furthermore, for those in high school who were tracked in general education, and after graduation found themselves in a rice field in southeast Asia fighting a war in a place that they could not even locate on a map, a connection with what was taught and their lives could have possibly made a difference between reading about a war and actually fighting one. They might have possibly joined the ranks of the privileged who went on to college and avoided being drafted. For those who did not speak the English language and who found themselves in classes of retarded children, when just a short time before in Puerto Rico they were on the honor roll, multicultural education would have recognized their uniqueness and would have used their mother tongue in making the transition from Spanish to English. Their years wasted in classes for retarded children, negative labeling, and a lifetime of self-doubt, insecurities, and the feelings of not being good enough that accompany such an experience might have been prevented. More importantly, the inadequate education resulting from years of little content learning received at the hands of teachers who wished to help without knowing how to could have been avoided. Even more dismal is the fact that some of these children became adults without being proficient in any language.

While multicultural education is not a panacea for all that ails the education system, it is broad and inclusive enough to address much of what is not working. We commend schools that have acknowledged the value of a multicultural education. They have provided hope to our young and thus strengthen the future of all.

Epilogue

This book traces the formal educational history of the Rubal sisters: kindergarten in the 1950s through a master's program in guidance and counseling in the early 1970s. Both sisters are in their twenties when the book ends. Their formal education, however, did not end here. Both sisters later, in their forties, received another master's degree in psychology and a doctoral degree in developmental psychology and linguistics. Angie also attended a theological seminary and became an ordained minister.

Needless to say, many things have occurred that extend beyond the time covered in the book. Life provides its own education and opportunities for personal and spiritual learning. Alma and Angie's parents divorced; Manolo remarried twice and became a widower after both wives died. Carmen became ill with arthritis once again and was paralyzed for eleven years prior to her death. The sisters shared in her caretaking. Fortunately, Carmen got to see grandchildren before her passing. Angie had a son and two marriages that ended in divorce. Alma had two daughters and has a stable marriage. Both currently work in higher education.

Educational achievement and formal and informal learning have continued to play an important role in their lives.

They both feel extremely grateful to affirmative action initiatives, which gave them the opportunity not only to study but also to work in higher education. As children, the idea of being a professor was outside the realm of their aspirations. It was inconceivable. They are aware that many of the opportunities afforded them resulted from the struggle of many courageous beings who fought for these opportunities. In particular, they have been inspired by the struggles of the American civil rights movement and the fight for Puerto Rican independence.

Both sisters have spent most of their professional careers in education hoping to widen the horizons of youngsters similar to themselves. They have tried to instill in young people a sense of giving back and not forgetting from whence they came.

Conclusion

Angie

How would I fare as a Puerto Rican/Nuyorican student in to-day's school system?

That is a very interesting and complex question. Like all children, I experienced pain and wounding in the process of grow-ing up. Much of this pain was related to being a Puerto Rican who went to school in the New York of the 1950s. Feelings of shame, a sense of inferiority and isolation, and a lack of confidence troubled me throughout much of my schooling. Ethnicity became a salient factor in my development.

Paradoxically, I was made to feel that I was inferior and at the same time exceptional and special. I was perceived as being unlike other Puerto Ricans. Ironically, my being unique and accepted de-pended on my capacity to reject my ethnic legacy. I developed great shame about being Puerto Rican, about feeling happy that I was per-ceived as special, and later about having internalized the negative stereotypes ascribed to my ethnic group.

I felt that I was very much on display. I felt the pressure to live up to the expectations of teachers, family, and friends. This resulted in my taking on the responsibility of being a role model. The term *role model* was used a lot when I was growing up. And I took this responsibility very seriously. Being a role model became a part of the agenda for every educational and career challenge I undertook. I still take being a role model seriously. I am very much aware of the fact that I am the first Hispanic woman to be a SEEK director at Baruch College. I never have accepted an assignment or position at the college without considering its impact on the advancement of people of color in general and of Hispanics in particular. It is like a reflex reaction.

I also felt like a token. I believed that my being hired at the college was very much related to my ethnicity. I was hired in the seventies to work with SEEK students who were primarily black and Hispanic and to help the college fulfill a racial quota. I also happened to be competent, credentialed, and hardworking. All the same, I recognize that many of the assignments at the college were allocated to me in large measure because of my being Hispanic. As a former Baruch president candidly expressed, he selected me to be on his commission because I was a Hispanic and a woman. This balanced out his committee on two counts—gender and ethnicity. Two tokens for the price of one!

On college committees, I served most often as a spokesperson for issues and concerns that were important to Hispanics. This does not mean that I could not and did not make other contributions while I was serving on these committees, but there seemed to be an unwritten expectation in terms of my role in these proceedings. Part of this was my own mind-set, which was focused on being responsible to my community and "giving back." I think this notion was true for many Hispanics of my generation and other people of color who were affirmative action babies. "Giving back" was a kind of mantra. It came with the territory.

In the early days, a natural alliance formed between the few African American and Latino faculty on campus. We stuck together. I felt that I belonged. Looking back, I think that if you were a faculty of color it was expected that you would take on several responsibilities. One was to be a role model. Another was to be an advocate for students of color. There were few black and Hispanic students in the early years at Baruch, and part of our mission was to assist these students in getting through the bureaucracy and density of the system.

We functioned as gatekeepers as well. Our role was to make sure that minority faculty were hired and retained. We served as a reminder that there was a social and human agenda as well as an academic one. There was strength in unity. We spoke with one voice and with clear purpose. If you did not assume these responsibilities, you were shunned as an opportunist who was concerned only about yourself and not about the common struggle. Thus, I lived under an added set of expectations, this time from my peers.

"Giving back" became a mission for me. I wanted to provide students with what I never got during my education. Even after thirty-two years of service at the college and now as an administrator, I continue to assume the role of mentor not only to students but also to junior staff. I do this because I realize how much I could have used a mentor during my youth. I would have been so happy to have had someone like myself instruct me or counsel me. I know that my life would have been very different. I made so many mistakes and wrong choices because I did not have an experienced person to bounce things off or to give me practical advice.

Today, as I look at the student body at Baruch College, I am amazed at the ethnic and racial diversity; there are so many students of color. Baruch boasts the most diverse campus in the United States. The Hispanics represent more than 25 percent of the college population. New York is a Latino town and it is cool to be Hispanic. Hispanic students are no longer isolated.

I can only imagine what it must be like to feel that you are not different. There is a Japanese saying: The nail that stands out gets hammered. To blend in and not to be alone is what looks so appealing to me when I think of going to school today. Loneliness is something that I felt for most of my educational process. The closest experience I had to feeling that I belonged was going to school in Puerto Rico. It was a relaxed and enjoyable time in my life.

The trade-off, of course, would have been not being regarded as unique or special. Being singled out as special can serve as a motivation or an incentive, as a self-fulfilling prophecy. In my case, I think it came at too high a cost. Although I had a natural love of learning, achievement became so embedded with issues of self-esteem and acceptance that I am not sure how my life would have been shaped without the pressure to succeed.

I am reminded of this when I speak to SEEK graduates who leave New York to pursue graduate studies on campuses with few blacks or Hispanic students. Some reside on campuses where the racism and prejudice are blatant and the cultural misunderstandings are many. The pain in these situations is clear. But even if the intolerance of the community is minimal or covert, many of the difficulties these students report are reminiscent of my experience. The sheer numbers of non-Hispanic students make them stand out. They share feelings of isolation and self-doubt, as well as the pressure of having to prove themselves.

These students, who did well academically in New York, often have great difficulty adjusting to these out-of-state institutions and communities and drop out. Those who make it through develop a great inner strength. Many describe having a new consciousness of who they are within the American society.

Going to school in today's New York would mean that my ethnicity would not have shaped so much of my life. I think that my ethnic wounding would have been less. These days, many students have less difficulty with embracing their ethnic and racial heritage and still identify themselves as being American. The celebration of differences has replaced the melting pot of my day. Today's multicultural academic curriculums would have allowed me to learn and appreciate more of my heritage. Self-acceptance and self-confidence might have come sooner in an environment that was more approving and tolerant. I might have trusted myself more and I might not have felt so obligated to live up to others' expectations. I certainly would have had more freedom to explore other paths.

Alma

The one question that surfaced throughout the course of writing this book was whether or not our experiences as Nuyorican children would be different today. To respond to this issue, I turned to my daughters for answers. How are their lives different from Angie's and my childhoods? How do they see themselves? How are they seen by their friends and the community at large? In contemplating this, I recollected a recent incident during a Puerto Rican Day Parade when my younger daughter's Egyptian friend came to my home dressed with Puerto Rican flags adorning her from head to toe. When asked why she was dressed like this, my daughter responded, "Everyone wants to be Puerto Rican, ma."

At that moment Angie and I looked at one another and knew that as adolescents this was never part of our experience. In fact, the opposite was true. Every cue, message, or image that we were exposed to, home notwithstanding, was one of depicting what we were as inferior and undesirable. We were not in the norm and therefore "not normal." Our small numbers, when out of our community, as well as our newness led to this undesirable categorization. Nonetheless, this status has changed, and during our respective childhoods the numbers of Puerto Ricans in the city of New York increased from 61,463 to 612,574. During this time, the Puerto Rican population represented 80.9 percent of the Latino population of the city. To be Latino was in essence to be Puerto Rican in New York. Nonetheless, the presence of Puerto Ricans compared to the remainder of the city's population was miniscule. As the Puerto Rican population continued to grow during the 1980s, so did the population of other Latinos.

This alteration in demographics was the result of the change in immigration laws during the 1960s, which has subsequently changed the population of the United States from a nation that was predominantly white and European to one with a significant population of persons of color. As the numbers of Dominicans, Central Americans, and South Americans increased, the number of Puerto Ricans also increased, but their percentage within the Latino group decreased. In the 1990s Puerto Ricans represented 50.3 percent of the Latino population, down from the previously cited 80.9 percent. Nonetheless, we continued to be seen as the prominent Latino group in New York City because of our presence in political and community domains, where we paved the way for future Hispanic groups.

For many who were ignorant of the differences between Latinos, any person with a Hispanic surname was automatically considered Puerto Rican. While this situation presented a problem for Puerto Ricans when depicted as welfare recipients, criminals, and the unemployed, it served to strengthen our leadership and pioneer role within the Latino community. The magnitude of the Latino presence was felt in every borough of New York, from the Colombian presence in Queens and the Dominican population in Manhattan to the growing numbers of Mexicans and Central Americans in parts of Brooklyn and the Bronx.

On the national level, the Latino presence became significant, with the increase of persons from all parts of Latin America in respective geographic areas of the Southeast, Southwest, and Northeast. What this increase in the number of Latinos did for the

Puerto Rican population is to underscore their presence and their importance in paving the way for those who followed, particularly in New York City.

In essence, to some extent the strength in numbers has allowed for children born within the past twenty years in New York City to be more the norm rather than the exception. The importance of this cannot be overemphasized because for children, particularly for adolescents, being like others is a very important factor in the development of their self-esteem. As young children leave their parents and head toward their initial experiences in school, their peers become increasingly important in shaping how they feel about themselves, in creating judgments about "others," and in the formation of their moral development. Our children have been fortunate that they have been born in a city and at a time that facilitate a good sense of who they are. This has allowed for an absence of shame and self-hate that easily emerge in an environment in which you are constantly told that you are not good enough. For a child, the mere thought that one is different is oftentimes interpreted as "not good enough." The absence of such thoughts I would say is the greatest difference between our childhoods and those of our children.

The presence of nonwhite non-Latinos in New York City has also helped to alleviate the feeling of anomie that often accompanies being the only one. The great increase in the numbers of persons from Asia, Africa, and the Caribbean has helped to change the norm to one that includes persons of color. Nonetheless, there have been times in the midst of this tremendously diverse metropolis when my children have experienced negative reactions for not being white. Such experiences have occurred when they were attending schools that were predominantly white or when living in a neighborhood with few children of color. Once again, being the "only one" or being "different" works against the minority population. Nonetheless, because of their strong sense of who they are, they have been able to overcome any stigma associated with being in the minority.

While a large Latino and racially diverse presence in New York City has helped to alleviate many of the challenges that we both experienced as young persons and thus improve the course of growing up for Latino children, it has lessened the pain of this experience only to some degree. Numbers do not translate into power, and therefore on an institutional level numbers alone cannot guarantee significant change.

For example, the Latino presence in the New York public schools has, undoubtedly, impacted on the teaching of children. In particular, the Latino presence has led to an increase in the population of children for whom English is not their first language. This has resulted in accommodations instituted for English language learners. Our institutions are currently to some extent better equipped to handle populations of new immigrants than they were when we were children. Angie's lack of English fluency during her initial school experience, for example, would have most likely been addressed with some support for English language learners rather than the "swim or sink" method that she experienced. Nonetheless, these changes that have emerged due to the Latino presence are not enough and are very often instituted by persons who know nothing about second-language learning.

Approximately forty years after the first significant group of Puerto Ricans were educated in New York public schools, we find that there is still a failure to adequately address the educational needs of Latinos. This failure is reflected in the low academic achievement of Latinos in New York as well as similar scores on the national level. Currently, we are the lowest academic achievers of all groups. Mexicans and Puerto Ricans lead other major Latino groups in their significant high school dropout rates and low representation in higher education.

The tracking of Latino students in general programs as we knew it—resulting in dead-end careers after high school—has been discontinued. Nonetheless, other obstacles that stand in the way of providing an equitable education to students of color in New York City have emerged. The raising of standards for a population educated in schools without certified teachers, with overcrowded classrooms, and often with inadequate facilities, leads to further failure, which subsequently results in issues of low self-esteem, learned helplessness, and ultimately an increase in dropouts. The commercial, academic, and general programs that we were familiar with as children do not exist. However, what does exist is a system that tracks children as gifted and talented or as children with special needs. The overwhelming population of children of color classified as needing special education sets the course of their educational career along a path of once again "being different," "being incapable," and "not in the norm." Moreover, the lack of qualified teachers to teach such a population only exacerbates the problem.

Not surprisingly, the overwhelming numbers of schools that are low performing are also predominantly black and Latino. This segregation of low-performing schools in New York City is easily seen when we examine the recent closings of various high schools due to a history of poor performance. Each and every one of these high schools is overwhelmingly populated by African American and Latino students.

As a mother of two daughters who has attempted to have them educated in public schools but was unsuccessful, I can honestly say that I have firsthandedly experienced how children are housed in ways that are not equitable. I have witnessed and experienced this discrepancy in ways that have made me feel rage such as I have rarely felt. After having my children attend a Montessori School for two years as young children, I had them tested and was told by my school district that they could accommodate my younger daughter in kindergarten in a gifted program but they could not accommodate my older child because of a lack of space. I therefore went to another district and had them privately tested as required by that district and had them both placed in gifted classes. When I called my home district to let them know that my younger child would not be attending because I was able to place both children in one school, they blocked my children from attending that school and forced both my girls to attend the home district.

Suddenly, they found room in a gifted program for both my daughters. Nonetheless, this gifted program was located in the district's lowest-performing school, with a segment of the population being children with severe behavioral problems, in one of the borough's poorest neighborhoods. To my surprise, on the first day of school, I noticed that most of the students in both my children's classes were children of color. This I found unusual, because if in fact this was a true gifted class, the population should have been more equally distributed by race. Such a skewed presence of children of color in a predominantly white district (although the school was located in a predominantly black and Hispanic area) would denote that in this district the only children who were gifted, with the exception of a few white children, were African American children and Latinos. In essence, it would mean that the only gifted children in this district were children of color. As a psychologist, I knew that this was statistically wrong, and so upon further investigation I found out that there was another gifted program in a white neighborhood that was composed mainly of white children with a small presence of children of color.

When I found out about this program, I inquired about the possibility of my children attending, since my work location was closer to this school. I was told that only children with an IQ of 140 and above could attend this program. Apparently, my daughter's score of 138 was not good enough. Knowing what I do about IQ scores and the distribution of such scores, I knew that this was a smokescreen for placing children where the powers that be wish to place them. What they were saying to me was that only white kids score higher than 140, and that a two-point difference on IQ tests makes a world of difference in the classroom. What I say to this is "bullshit."

In this district, the tracking of children in these programs had become a way of providing a shelter for white kids from children of color. Not only was the overwhelming number of children of color in one class in an overwhelmingly white district an indication that these gifted classes were not really what they were, but there were other obvious clues. For example, my daughter sat next to a child who talked to himself the entire day and very rarely interacted with anyone. He was physically dirty and smelled in a horrible way, an indication that this child was not being properly taken care of at home. Although I have no way of knowing what was really wrong with this child, his lack of interaction with the rest of the children and his immersion in his own little world would lead me to believe that he might have been autistic. More importantly, his inability to keep up with the class would be a further indication that he was improperly placed in this class. When students would leave these gifted classes because they moved or because their parents realized the inadequacy of such schooling, children from the general population, without having any testing, would be placed in these classes, further attesting to the lie that these classes were in fact for gifted children. Although after two years I gave up and withdrew my children from public school, I was able to keep track of the academic lives of many of these children through the continual associations of my daughters with their former classmates. Not surprisingly, only a few of these children made it into the most competitive junior high schools, a further indication of the bogusness of these gifted classes. In essence, these parents had been lied to about the kind of education that their kids were receiving. The discrepancy between what a gifted program is and what my girls' classes were was unknowingly substantiated by my daughter's kindergarten teacher, during a conversation that we had during a class trip. She was informing me about the great schools her children attended in a predominantly white neighborhood of Staten Island. When I informed her that I had briefly (very briefly) contemplated the possibility of moving to this area because of my husband's work location in New Jersey, she quickly intercepted me and told me that my children would have to be retested in order to be placed in gifted classes, implying that once they left this school their so-called "gifted" status would cease to exist. In essence, they were gifted enough for this black and Hispanic class but not gifted enough for her children's white school. In essence, "giftedness" in certain schools in New York City is defined differently.

When my younger child went to high school, I was able to use my contacts to have her placed in a high-performing secondary school. My being a faculty member of a major school of education afforded my having these contacts. Sadly to say, in the ten years since my negative experience with gifted classes, little had changed. This supposedly "good school," which was supposed to be populated by a lottery system, was ethnically and racially skewed in favor of whites, in particular, Russians. This was a very good school, but access to the population at large was not occurring. Yes, the school does have students of color, but the composition of the student body leads me to conclude that the randomness that is supposed to exist in the selection of students is not occurring. My experience in the domain of public education has allowed me to witness firsthand how numbers alone do not guarantee equity.

The fact that our children have been born to professional parents has set the dynamics for our children to be the "only ones" on occasion during their lives. My daughters were enrolled in a small, private Catholic school that was overwhelmingly Irish and Italian. When negative comments about persons of color were made, I was able to explain that such comments came from ignorance and a lack of education. The fact that such things would never be said in our home about anyone I attributed to the fact that we know better. This is not to say that educated persons are not racist, but this was used as a possible reason for racism and as an opportunity to turn the disadvantage of being in the minority to a positive thing. I would quickly inform my daughters that being a loan shark and living in a million-dollar house, as some of their classmates' parents were and did, could not take away the fact that some of their classmates came from uneducated families. The fact that my children were the only children of a mother with a Ph.D. and a father who was an attorney turned the tides of power for my daughters. In this case, the Puerto Rican was the more educated. This, however, did not prevent the rejection as well as the loneliness that at times both girls felt while attending this school. In this particular institution, incidents of this kind repeatedly reminded me of the disadvantages and destructiveness of being the "one and only," and further made me realize that many years later the same racist dynamics in a so-called "religious" institution still permeated the culture of that domain. I found myself having to constantly instill in my children the fact that they were someone in order to counteract the pernicious impact that other children's racist views could ultimately have on my children's lives. I had become my mother, protecting my children from the evils of racism.

As children of immigrants, one of the greatest problems that Angie and I faced was the great cultural distance between our family and the rest of the population. Our customs, food, manner of dress, language, and values were quite different from those of our peers. When we migrated to Puerto Rico, we faced a tremendous difference in the ways we lived as compared to those on the island, as well as a lack of acceptance by many. During this time, Puerto Rico was in the initial stages of modernization. In today's society, one could say that there still exists a cultural distance, but that gap has been narrowed by technology. With Puerto Ricans, this cultural gap becomes narrower and narrower with every new generation. The quick and intense change in Puerto Rico from a rural agrarian society to an urbanized nation has resulted in a population with excellent access to American media, resulting in citizens with knowledge about American culture. Air travel has also facilitated travel to and from Puerto Rico and has, thus, contributed to the narrowing of the cultural gap between the island of Puerto Rico and the mainland. More importantly, the presence of the use of English in official domains of education as well as in financial and legal areas has further contributed to closing the gap.

For example, it is not unusual for people to choose to do their tertiary education on the mainland. The fact that one can go from twelve years of education on the island and compete in major universities in the United States without having a significant language problem attests to the middle-class knowledge of English. This is not to say that everyone on the island is fluent in English, but it is not uncommon for private schools to use English as the medium of instruction (a desired educational choice for the growing middle class). In addition, many public schools have an adequate English-language program where English is taught as a subject rather than used as a medium of instruction.

Moreover, the travel from Puerto Rico to the United States has become so fluid that the distinction between Puerto Rican and Nuyorican in many instances is impossible to make. It is common to meet Puerto Ricans who have lived for a few years in Puerto Rico, then have migrated to the United States, and have continued this pattern throughout their lives. They are able to adapt to both places without much of a problem. Furthermore, as one of the foremost importers of United States exports, Puerto Rican consumers indulge themselves very much like Americans do. This includes shopping at the endless number of malls around the island—which include stores like Macy's, Home Depot, Wal-Mart, Sears, and J.C. Penney—as well as consuming foods from McDonald's, Wendy's, KFC, Church, Pizza Hut, and Burger King, to mention just a few of the endless array of fast foods commonly found throughout the island.

For children relocating from Puerto Rico to the United States, this prior knowledge about American culture is advantageous. On the other hand, it is comforting for the child who is relocating to Puerto Rico. In essence, the gap has been lessened, making the adaptation easier. Nonetheless, the impact of this consumerism, as well as the infiltration of American pop culture on the values and culture of Puerto Ricans, is in many ways devastating.

Our childhood experience of living in a rural community and cows entering our classroom would now not happen except in a very remote area of Puerto Rico. In fact, that small town of Trujillo Alto where we went to school has become a densely populated bedroom community easily accessible by car or bus.

One domain in which the Latino presence has emerged is in the media. The likes of Jennifer Lopez, Ricky Martin, and Mark Anthony help to remind everyone that there is a significant presence of Latinos in the United States. Nonetheless, these are just a few in a huge industry that in turn reminds us that although there is a presence of Puerto Ricans, the power is not held by us. Such a phenomenon exists not only in the media but in every aspect of American life as well. Even on a national level, where the Latino presence is significant and leads as the largest minority group, our presence in positions of power is insignificant. In New York City and state, for example, where the Latino student population is overwhelmingly great, there is a lack of a strong presence of Latinos in positions where policy is created. If one counts the number of commissioners, assistant commissioners, superintendents, regents, and so on, one realizes how very few people of color make up this select group. In essence, numbers do not necessarily translate into power.

After contemplating the original question regarding whether our experiences growing up as Nuyorican children would be different today, I would definitely have to say that many of our experiences would be very similar. These experiences will continue to exist as long as racism exists. Nonetheless, the feeling of being the only one would be less common and usually confined to an extremely segregated situation, a fairly uncommon occurrence in a city like New York. In essence, the Latino presence has not altered the disadvantages that accompany being poor, nonwhite, and a linguistic minority, but it has provided company in this misery. It also has brought us hope. If one looks at the projected demographics, we (the Latinos) represent the future of this nation. Our success will in turn be the success of this nation, and our failure will also be its downfall. In essence, we are the future United States

References

Agueros, J. (1991). Halfway to Dick and Jane. In C. J. Verburg (Ed.), *Ourselves among others: Cross-cultural readings for writers* (95–112). New York: St. Martin's Press.

Anselmo, A. (1992). Language and culture: The struggle between hegemony and humanism. In A. Lorenzo, C. F. Junquera, & J. A. Palacios (Eds.), *El poder Hispano* (pp. 305–312). Madrid: Universidad de Alcala.

Arce, C. A. (1981) A reconsideration of Chicano culture and identity. *Daedalus*, 110, 177–192.

Atkinson, D. R., Morten, G., & Sue, D. W. (Eds). (1989). *Counseling American minorities: A cross-cultural perspective* (4th ed.). Dubuque, IA: William C. Brown.

Atkinson, D. R., Thompson, C. E., & Grant, S. K. (1993). A three-dimensional model for counseling racial/ethnic minorities. *The Counseling Psychologist*, 21, 257–277.

Banks, James A. (2002). *An introduction to multicultural education.* Boston: Allyn & Bacon.

Brophy, Jere. (1998). *Motivating students to learn.* New York: McGraw-Hill.

Cross, W. E. (1991). *Shades of black: Diversity in African-American identity.* Philadelphia: Temple University Press.

Darling-Hammond, L. (1997). Education for democracy. In W. C. Ayers & J. L. Miller (Eds.), *A light in dark times: Maxine Greene and the unfinished conversation* (pp. 78–92). New York: Teachers College Press.

Deci, E., & Ryan, R. (1991). A motivational approach to self: Integration in personality. In R. Dienstbier (Ed.), *Nebraska symposium on motivation, Volume 38: Perspectives on motivation* (pp. 237–288). Lincoln: University of Nebraska Press.

Deci, E., & Ryan, R. (1994). Promoting self-determined education. *Scandinavian Journal of Educational Research*, 38, 3–14.

Delpit, L. (1995). *Other people's children: Cultural conflict in the classroom.* New York: The New Press.

Donaldson, K. (1994). Through students' eyes. *Multicultural Education,* 2, 2 (December), 26–28.

Edmonds, R. (1986). Characteristics of effective schools. In U. Neisser (Ed.), *The school achievement of minority children: New perspectives* (pp. 237–288). Hillsdale, NJ: Lawrence Erlbaum.

Erikson, E. H. (1950). *Childhood and society.* New York: Norton.

Erikson, E. H. (1968). *Identity: Youth and crisis.* New York: Norton.

Flores, J., Attinasi, J., and Pedraza, P. (1981). La carreta made a u-turn: Puerto Rican language and culture in the United States. *Daedalus* (Spring), 193–238.

Gilyard, K. (1991). *Voices of the self: A study of language competence.* Detroit: Wayne State University Press.

Grumet, M. (1996). The curriculum: What are the basics and are we teaching them? In J. Kincheloe & S. Steinberg (Eds.), *Thirteen questions: Reframing education's conversation.* New York: Peter Lang.

Haberman, M. (1991). The poverty of poverty versus good teaching. *Phi Delta Kappan,* 73, 4.

Hale, J. E. (2001). *Learning while black: Creating educational excellence for African American children.* Baltimore: Johns Hopkins University Press.

Hillard, A. G. (1988). Conceptual confusion and the persistence of group oppression through education. *Equity and Excellence in Education,* 24, 1, 45–67.

Hollingsworth, S. (1997). Social responsibility and imagination: Lessons and letters. In W. C. Ayers & J. L. Miller (Eds.), *A light in dark times: Maxine Greene and the unfinished conversation.* New York: Teachers College Press.

hooks, b. (1994). *Teaching to transgress: Education as the practice of freedom.* New York: Routledge.

Irizarry, N. L. (1981). *Parental goals in a fishing village.* Unpublished doctoral dissertation, Harvard University, Boston.

Kim, J. (1981). *Process of Asian-American identity development: A study of Japanese American women's perceptions of their struggle to achieve positive identities.* Unpublished doctoral dissertation, University of Massachusetts, Amherst.

Kincheloe, J., Slattery, P., & Steinberg, S. (2000). *Contextualizing teaching.* New York: Longman.

Kozol, J. (1992). *Savage inequalities: Children in America's schools.* New York: Harper Perennial.

Kozol, J. (1995). *Amazing grace: Lives of children and the conscience of a nation*. New York : Harper Collins

Ladson-Billings, G. (1994). *The dreamkeepers: Successful teachers of African American children*. San Francisco: Jossey-Bass.

Lasker, B. (1929). *Race attitudes in children*. New York: Holt.

Lewis, M. (1996). Power and education: Who decides the forms schools have taken, and who should decide? In J. Kincheloe & S. Steinberg (Eds.), *Thirteen questions: Reframing education's conversation* (pp. 33–43, part 1). New York: Peter Lang.

Macedo, D. (1994). *Literacies of power*. Boulder, CO: Westview Press.

Macedo, D. (1996). Power and education: Who decides the forms schools have taken, and who should decide? In J. Kincheloe & S. Steinberg (Eds.), *Thirteen questions: Reframing education's conversation* (pp. 43–59, part 2). New York: Peter Lang.

Mahiri, J. (1998). *Shooting for excellence: African American and youth culture in new century schools*. New York: Teachers College Press.

Meek, A. (1989). On creating ganas: A conversation with Jaime Escalante. *Educational Leadership* 46, no. 5, 46.

Newman, J. W. (1996). Socioeconomic class and education: In what ways does class affect the educational processes? In J. Kincheloe & S. Steinberg (Eds.), *Thirteen questions: Reframing education's conversation* (pp. 193–205). New York: Peter Lang.

Nieto, S. (1996). *Affirming diversity: The sociopolitical context of multicultural education*. New York: Longman.

Nieto, S. (1997). On becoming American: An exploratory essay. In W. C. Ayers & J. L. Miller (Eds.), *A light in dark times: Maxine Greene and the unfinished conversation* (pp. 45–57). New York: Teachers College Press.

Oakes, J. (1992). Can tracking research inform practice? Technical, normative, and political considerations. *Educational Researcher*, 21 (4), 12–21.

Ogbu, J. U. (1994). From cultural differences to differences in cultural frames of reference. In P. M. Greenfield & R. R. Cockings (Eds.), *Cross-cultural roots of minority child development* (pp. 365–391). Hillsdale, NJ: Lawrence Erlbaum.

Phinney, J. S. (1989). Stages of ethnic identity in minority group adolescence. *Journal of Early Adolescence*, 9, 34–49.

Phinney, J. S. (1990). Ethnic identity in adolescents and adults. Review of research. *Psychological Bulletin*, 108, 499–514.

Phinney, J. S. & Alipuria, L. (1990). Ethnic identity in older adolescents from four ethnic groups. *Journal of Adolescence*, 13, 171–183.

Phinney, J. S., Lochner, B. T., & Murphy, R. (1990). Ethnic identity development and psychological adjustment in adolescence. In A. R. Stiffman & L. B. Davis (Eds.), *Ethnic issues in adolescent mental health* (pp. 274–292). Newbury Park, CA: Sage.

Phinney, J. S., & Tarver, S. (1988). Ethnic identity search and commitment in black and white eighth graders. *Journal of Early Adolescence*, 8, 265–277.

Pinar, W. F. (1996). The curriculum: What are the basics and are we teaching them? In J. Kincheloe & S. Steinberg (Eds.), *Thirteen questions: Reframing education's conversation*. New York: Peter Lang.

Rodriguez, C. (1991). *Puerto Ricans born in the United States*. Boulder, CO: Westview Press.

Rubal-Lopez, A. (1992). *The linguistic acculturation of Puerto Ricans in the United States*. In A. Lorenzo, C. F. Junquera, & J. A. Palacios (Eds.), *El poder Hispano* (pp. 327–337). Madrid: Universidad de Alcala.

Spencer, M. B. (2001). Identity, achievement orientation, and race: "Lessons learned" about the normative developmental experiences of African American males. In W. H. Watkins, J. H. Lewis, & V. Chou (Eds.), *Race & education: The roles of history and society in educating African American students* (pp. 100–123). Boston: Allyn & Bacon.

Stanley, W. (1996). Socioeconomic class and education: In what ways does class affect the educational processes? In J. Kincheloe & S. Steinberg (Eds.), *Thirteen questions: Reframing education's conversation* (pp 205–215). New York: Peter Lang.

Steinberg, L. (1998). *Beyond the classroom*. New York: Simon & Schuster.

Steinberg, S., & Kincheloe, J. (1997). *Kinderculture*. Boulder, CO: Westview Press.

Stonequist, E. V. (1961). *The marginal man: A study in personality and culture conflict*. New York: Russell & Russell.

Taylor, D., & Dorsey-Gaines, C. (1988). *Growing up literate: Learning from inner-city families*. Portsmouth, NH: Heinemann.

Villanueva, V. (1993). *Bootstraps from an American academic of color*. Urbana, IL: National Council of Teachers of English.

Zentella, A. (1997). *Growing Up Bilingual: Puerto Rican Children in New York*. Malden, MA: Blackwell.

Studies in the Postmodern Theory of Education

General Editors
Joe L. Kincheloe & Shirley R. Steinberg

Counterpoints publishes the most compelling and imaginative books being written in education today. Grounded on the theoretical advances in criticalism, feminism, and postmodernism in the last two decades of the twentieth century, Counterpoints engages the meaning of these innovations in various forms of educational expression. Committed to the proposition that theoretical literature should be accessible to a variety of audiences, the series insists that its authors avoid esoteric and jargonistic languages that transform educational scholarship into an elite discourse for the initiated. Scholarly work matters only to the degree it affects consciousness and practice at multiple sites. Counterpoints' editorial policy is based on these principles and the ability of scholars to break new ground, to open new conversations, to go where educators have never gone before.

For additional information about this series or for the submission of manuscripts, please contact:

Joe L. Kincheloe & Shirley R. Steinberg
c/o Peter Lang Publishing, Inc.
275 Seventh Avenue, 28th floor
New York, New York 10001

To order other books in this series, please contact our Customer Service Department:

(800) 770-LANG (within the U.S.)
(212) 647-7706 (outside the U.S.)
(212) 647-7707 FAX

Or browse online by series:

www.peterlangusa.com